Praise for *Lead by l*

One of the cardinal principles of effective leadership is that you cannot lead where you will not go. In her instructive and inspiring book on leadership, Sheila Robinson shares her own story of going against the odds to achieve success in corporate America and the world of entrepreneurship. No easy task for an African American woman! In *Lead by Example*, Sheila Robinson convincingly demonstrates that if she could do it, so can women of diverse communities and cultures.

Johnnetta Betsch Cole, Ph.D.
President Emerita of Spelman College and
Bennett College for Women

Sheila Robinson is the epitome of leading by example. As a successful mentor, entrepreneur, and consummate business professional, she shares life-changing strategies and tips that are relevant to women of all cultures, backgrounds, and levels. You are sure to be set up for success in your career and in life after you read *Lead by Example*.

Shirley Davis Sheppard, Ph.D., SPHR
Global Workforce and Talent Management Expert,
and CEO of The Success Doctor, LLC

Sheila Robinson doesn't just teach you how to lead...she leads by example. This book provides invaluable advice from her experiences as well as those of women who are entrepreneurs, midlevel managers, and corporate executives from the nation's leading companies. An invaluable resource for modern women and our global business world.

Dr. Frances Hesselbein
President and CEO of the Frances Hesselbein Leadership Institute
and Presidential Medal of Honor Recipient

Lead By Example demonstrates, through the power of practice and example, the innumerable benefits corporations gain when women are seated at the table of decision-making.

Steve Pemberton
Author and Divisional Vice President
and Chief Diversity Officer, Walgreens

Lead by Example

An Insider's Look At How To Successfully Lead in Corporate America and Entrepreneurship

SHEILA A. ROBINSON

Diversity Woman Media, LLC
USA

Lead by Example

An Insider's Look At How To Successfully Lead in Corporate America and Entrepreneurship

Published by
Diversity Woman Media, LLC
1183 University Drive
Suite 105131
Burlington, NC 27215
http://diversitywoman.com
(336) 543-0644

First Edition: January 2014
Printed in the United States of America
ISBN: 978-0-9916582-0-6
Library of Congress Control Number: 2014935340

Cover design by Cathy Krizik
Interior design and layout by Juanita Dix

Table of Contents

I would like to acknowledge my family and all the wise and wonderful men and women who have supported me throughout the decades of my professional and personal journey. Their unconditional love, ready support and heartfelt service helped make me who I am today.

Introduction

As far back as I can remember, I have always been an advocate for the career advancement of women of all races, cultures and backgrounds. *Lead By Example* is the latest milestone in my journey, and I hope it will mark a new pathway for your own journey. In these pages I will share my experiences and the experiences of my fellow colleagues. My goal is not to give you checklists of must-haves and must-dos. I won't try to micromanage or control every aspect of your career, and I would never try to tell you what to do or how to do it. Instead, my promise to you and every reader of this book is this:

I will respect you.

I will honor you.

I will make suggestions and guide you based on my experiences and the insight I've gathered from dozens of women who hold leadership roles from start-ups to CEOs. I will encourage you to find your passion and live your dream. And I will be your first and most vocal supporter no matter where your journey takes you. If you find anything in this book that is useful or beneficial, it will give me joy. My mission is to support others in a way that prevents them from experiencing the negative pitfalls I encountered.

I say I'm not an expert because I believe that every woman has the ability to take on the same kind of leadership role as I already have. Whether you're an executive, an entrepreneur or just graduating from college, you have already led others. You might have never held a title that reflected your leadership duties, but you worked hard to get where you are in life. You also have the determination and persistence to go further. You have already shown your coworkers, neighbors and friends how powerful you are. You have already led by example.

We all have something to offer. What I'm offering you right now is insight into my own path. By the time I was forty-two, I had been laid off from three major corporations. During my parents' lives, those companies had guaranteed their workers financial security during their employment and into retirement. My idea of a perfect life was to spend my days at a job I loved then come home to take care of my family. After fruitless job hunts, I took the leap of faith to explore my vision for a career magazine that would help others.

Along the way I benefited by having access to other people's experience. I learned how to avoid certain challenges and how best to deal with those that threatened my progress. I discovered how passion and attitude impact my financial and personal returns on investment. And when I shared my experiences in ways that helped others achieve their own success, I reaped the deep satisfaction that comes from lifting up my fellow women.

Since I can't personally appear everywhere women need to hear my message of empowerment, daring and hope, I needed to reach out in a new way. This book is an important step forward because a book can reach people from Bangladesh to Bangor, Maine, and from London, England to Los Angeles, California. So I reached out to peers who hold leadership roles across the United States. The interviews I conducted with them, as well as articles and interviews culled from *Diversity Woman* magazine, provided my associates an opportunity to give back. The book you're holding in your hands today is the result.

My deepest wish is that *Lead by Example* is also an important step forward for you. Within these pages you'll see how women from every race, culture and background overcame adversity by turning each challenge into an opportunity. Every story is real, and is told by a real woman who is just like you. In their stories and successes, you'll recognize that you have the same innate strengths and abilities…and that you can also achieve the successes you have chosen for your own life.

You'll discover that a positive attitude and an unrelenting focus on doing the right thing will guide you through any crisis. During my time inside corporate America, I faced many adversities. I grew up in the South during an era when anyone outside the old boy network wasn't likely to break through to top earning positions. As a young woman willing to work hard to rise through the ranks, I took entry-level jobs that threatened to sabotage my dreams before they could fully blossom. And as an African American in a world dominated by white Americans, I truly have always had to be twice as good or ten times better than my peers. In order to beat those incredibly long odds, I had to use my knowledge and wisdom to create solutions.

Over the years, my basic equation has remained the same. Knowledge plus wisdom equals true power. Knowledge is reaped from new opportunities and stepping up to accept new challenges. Knowledge also comes from educating myself through formal schooling and informal channels like engaging with mentors. Wisdom is distilled from the days and months and years I spent pursuing my goals and dreams. The experiences I gained and the experiences my peers and mentors shared with me provided the insight I needed to build the life and lifestyle I enjoy today.

All of this knowledge and wisdom is contained in the chapters of this book. Together we'll celebrate how the myths about women in business have been shattered. We'll explore how the pallet offered by people of color, those who are visibly or invisibly disabled, members of the LGBT community, people of different ages, and those with differently sized bodies allow companies to innovate based on different perspectives. You'll be inspired to display an attitude that radiates real confidence, true power, and an energetic passion. You'll discover that persistence and determination are your best tools whether you're stepping into a new position or starting up your own business.

I also promise to believe in you. I know that you already believe enough in yourself to pick up this book. Your decision to invest precious time and effort into expanding your knowledge and enhancing your wisdom is powerful proof that you have what it takes to succeed. To build a life and a lifestyle that serves your goals, needs and desires, you must recognize the depth and breadth of your existing skills and abilities. You must believe deeply in the vision you hold, starting right now.

You also have to know yourself. You must understand your own motivation. You must define success on your own terms and align your passion with your values. You might be switching careers, seeking new job opportunities, taking on new challenges or enhancing your approach to your existing career path. No matter where you are at this moment, *Lead by Example* will take you farther than ever before. No matter what obstacles you face, you'll find someone in these pages who has triumphed against similar conditions. In their victory lies the example that will lead you to your own power.

By the end of this book, you'll have found inner strength. You'll know that you're worthy of success and that you deserve to achieve every goal you set for yourself. Real change will come from your attitude. When you present yourself as a capable, qualified person who believes in herself and in the abilities of other women, you create the world anew. Your powerful attitude shines through when you know who you truly are, when you trust your abilities and capabilities, when you align your values with your work. What you say and do reflects who you are...and who you are will create a joyful journey to your own fulfillment.

My role as the founder of Diversity Woman Media has provided me with that same joyful fulfillment. The opportunities I've been offered by following my passion are incredible. Over the years, I've met women from every sector of American business who stand at every level of corporate and personal success. The paths they have walked are as different as their personalities. This diversity is a thing of beauty, so embrace your personality and the path it guides you down. Celebrate each milestone for the richness and joy it creates in your life.

Nobody ever said the road to success is easy. Your celebrations are, I know, hard won. So in these pages, we'll take an unflinching look at the obstacles women still face in the world today. Sometimes the adversity I've encountered has felt like a storm. A few rained down more damage than I could have imagined, while others dissipated in threats that turned out to have been illusions. Even if a challenge changes your life forever, it's an opportunity to grow. *Lead by Example* will show you how innovative and creative problem-solving can help you build a different, better future for yourself, your company and your employees.

I've spent my life turning adversity into opportunity. Within a culture that didn't understand the real meaning of inclusion, I built *Diversity Woman* magazine into a publication that is now carried in Barnes & Noble stores across the nation. The value provided to my Twitter followers has created a feed that is trending #1 in diversity. The annual conference where I gather powerful speakers, executives and consultants has been recognized as the top leadership event in America.

Every year testimony pours in about how the workshops and presentations offered at the conference support and transform attendees' lives. The magazine has garnered similar praise from women of every race, culture and background. This book contains the same kind of advice, thoughts, tips and techniques embedded in the stories of real women who've been where you want to go. And because true inclusion welcomes everyone to the discussion, men who have made particular efforts to help women advance also speak in these pages.

Once you've read this book, share it with others. Reach out to other women. Take their hands and their hearts into your own. Together—truly together, fully together; male and female, abled and disabled, gay and straight, plus-size and skinny, white women and women of color, American-born and naturalized—we can allow everyone to bring their true selves into the workplace. Together we will encourage every individual's best performance and fire their passion. Together, we will lead each other with our own true example.

CHAPTER ONE

Turning Adversity
Into Opportunity

I'M A NORTH CAROLINA GIRl, and I think this state is one of the most beautiful places in America. If you've ever been here, you know the diversity of the natural environment: coastline, beaches and barrier islands, and saline estuaries that reach inland until they give way to the Sandhills. In the middle of the state, the fertile soil supports farmland and even vineyards. While natural beauty abounds, North Carolina also has its share of stormy weather. Hurricanes send nature lovers fleeing from the coast. Summer thunderstorms and winter ice snarls traffic, knocks out electricity, and brings daily living to an unexpected halt.

The storms are not all bad. The heavy ice that breaks trees also coats their branches like sparkling jewels. Snow storms that can damage homes blanket the ground in soft, white powder. Hurricanes and thunderstorms nurture crops and flowers. In a way, these weather patterns mirror the ups and downs of our daily lives. Sometimes we face difficulties that seem dark and stormy. Hurricanes

1

show up at work or home, fallen trees in the form of obstacles cause us to rethink our plans, and the ice storms of unexpected experiences threaten to send us sliding downhill. If the storm is especially challenging and goes on long enough, we might feel as if we'll break or fail or be swept away. But we don't have to be. No matter how bad it gets, we can survive.

Sometimes the adversity I've encountered has felt like a storm. The challenges I've faced have been as easily managed as a misty rain; others were more like all out, Level 4 hurricanes. A few did more damage than I could have imagined, while others left me relatively unscathed. After each storm I began the process of rebuilding my job, my career or my life...as everyone does. This chapter is about the life-giving rain that follows dark clouds and thunder. Adversity is difficult to bear but when it's all over, don't focus only on the past or the changes caused by the weather. Look around for the good. You just might discover that the storm has deposited something even better at your feet.

Teamwork Makes History

One of my most prominent adversities occurred while I was in high school. I know that high school happenings are often trivial, but this incident had a significant impact. In 1978, I was a member of the Parkland High School cheerleading squad. It was time for elections. The team—nine whites and four blacks—voted me in as their captain. This wouldn't have happened everywhere in the U.S. at the time, but these young women based their decision on my ability to lead, my personality, and my commitment to the squad. They put me in charge because of my ability without regard to my skin color.

The voting process was the same each year. The cheer coach, Mrs. Malcolm, polled each cheerleader privately for her choice, which pressured the students to support her own choice. That year, unbeknownst to me or the coach, my teammates had gotten together behind the scenes and planned how they would vote. They told Mrs. Malcolm what she wanted to hear then cast their votes for me. When the ballots were tallied, she turned beet red. And I soon learned that the vote was only the beginning of my difficulties.

Mrs. Malcolm challenged me the entire year. She denigrated my ideas and belittled our activities at every turn. Her rejection stung but the squad persevered. We ended up being one of the most forward-thinking cheerleading squads in the history of the school. For the first time, the squad attended the Cheerleader Spirit Conference to seek out new ideas. We were the first to do stunts and innovative halftime performances. Rather than let her contempt hinder our success, we made sure that the team and our performance always took priority. All our hard work paid off. Never before in the school's history had the cheer squad reached such heights.

The squad accomplished all this despite the challenges. One challenge that vividly stands out presented itself right away. At the beginning of football season, the local newspaper always ran a full-page color photo of the captains of the football team and cheerleading squad. Instead of calling me to the photo shoot, Coach Malcolm contacted the co-captain. We all knew that the co-captain had been her choice for captain, but this was beyond what I'd expected, even from her.

When the photo came out the coach claimed she'd had no way of getting in touch with me. That was just a pretext—she didn't want me to be in the picture. For me, as a teenage girl, the blow was devastating. I'd known I was dealing with discrimination, so her efforts to undermine me weren't a surprise. The behavior of the co-captain—my teammate—was more challenging. She chose to stand for the portrait, and to stand for everything the photo represented, which was my exclusion. It felt like a betrayal.

The school's administration never acknowledged any wrongdoing, nor did they offer any kind of an apology. Instead, rather than celebrating the school's advances in the racial sphere or correcting the coach's actions, they pretended like there had been no milestone to celebrate—or at least nothing important enough to spotlight for the larger community. For the rest of the year, I was determined to beat the coach at her own game. I became the best cheerleading captain I could be. Her public display of small-mindedness, arrogance, and the school's complicit silence couldn't stop me from improving myself and my team.

I'd like to say that the matter ended there, but the following year, Mrs. Malcolm changed how the vote was handled. The squad outsmarted her again and for the second year in a row, an African American student was elected team cheerleading captain based on her qualifications and abilities. We made sure that she was featured in the annual photo shoot. Despite the adversity, I was the first black cheerleading captain ever elected in the history of my predominantly white school. It was a historical milestone for my entire community. It's an accomplishment I'll always remember with pride.

Corporate Adversity

After being employed for several years, I landed a job I felt could provide significant career advancement opportunities. The marketing assistant role was at DuPont, a Fortune 500 company. I was thrilled about the job and convinced I was on my way up the corporate ladder. Until the day my supervisor informed me I would never be anything but a secretary. And I thought I was a marketing assistant! His comments were a surprise because in my mind I was working towards becoming a marketing representative. From his perspective, marketing representatives had engineering degrees. My B.A. wasn't going to cut it.

When I'd joined his organization, he'd clearly stated that his group offered little room for advancement. That should have been a red flag. I took the job because it was an entry-level position in a division that was difficult to access. I had a college degree and was a hard worker, so I figured that my qualifications and performance would change his mind. They didn't. I watched the company hire plenty of marketing representatives straight out of college. They were all younger, had less experience than I did, and none of them were African American. Not only was I facing the obstacle of my gender and of being a woman of color in a predominantly white male division, I had been stereotyped as support personnel. Administrative. Clerical. That turned out to be more challenging than being a woman of color!

So I decided to focus on my strengths. I was determined to use the experience I gained at the company to secure employment elsewhere. Before leaving, I would avail myself of their educational benefits and continuing education resources to pursue a graduate degree. I began taking marketing courses and continued to learn everything I could in my role. As soon as I took my focus off of the negative aspects of my situation and channeled my energy towards making a positive contribution, I became more effective. The marketing executives soon knew my name and accolades rolled in.

Despite this, my supervisor was unwilling to move me into a role with more responsibility. Then things changed. Less than a year after uttering those fateful words, my supervisor retired. My new supervisor had a vastly different perception of me. He began giving me marketing projects to handle, and even told me I would do well in marketing communications. To say that I was shocked would be an understatement!

It took some time, but he eventually promoted me into a salaried position as a marketing communications representative. Over the years I rose to the level of manager and was responsible for marketing communications. My role included managing a $300 thousand dollar budget and working with major brands like

Essence and Hanes Hosiery. I spent time with famous designers and celebrities, and eventually took charge of public relations for all the company's North American apparel business, a position in global and consumer branding.

My experiences at DuPont taught me that adversity is not the final word in my (or anyone else's) situation. We need to look at obstacles as opportunities in disguise and use them to find new paths to reach our goals. This doesn't mean we pretend that negative circumstances don't exist. Instead, we should acknowledge difficulties with a positive attitude and refuse to allow challenges to waylay our future. My professional career began with significant adversity, but through perseverance and patience, I was able to triumph. You can, too.

Leading Through Adversity

Most of the time you'll face adversity on a personal level. By that I mean you'll encounter situations on the job or as you build your business. The adversity might impact your coworkers or your employees in some way, but primarily you'll find that you need to take personal responsibility for facing that adversity. There are times, however, when adversity hits on a much larger scale. The events surrounding 9/11 are a poignant example.

Around that time, I was a trade show manager and was involved in a major exhibition in Miami. When the towers were hit, the entire country was stunned. Because the trade show was in Florida, the administrators decided not to cancel. As you might imagine, this was not a popular decision; people wanted to be with their loved ones during this crisis. I ended up running the company's portion of the show with a skeleton crew of three people. Even during extreme circumstances, we must attend to our responsibilities. We might not be given a break, and expectations might be placed on us that are upsetting in light of the circumstances.

Other women felt the pressure of 9/11 more acutely. Dr. Dana McDonald Mann is president of a consulting company that specializes in talent management. Before that, she was the senior vice president of executive development for a Fortune 500 company. On August 30 of that year, she left a lucrative consulting job to start her own business. After 9/11, her potential engagements disappeared and her business collapsed. "I found myself in the midst of an extremely dark cloud," Mann says. "The silver lining, if there was one, wasn't immediately obvious."

She began to explore her options. "With much creativity, a willingness to explore, and a willingness to reinvent myself, I wrote my own answer," she says. "Two years later I emerged in a new city as the proud mother of a nine-month-old daughter and the senior leader in a Fortune 50 financial institution." Mann used her creativity, her network and her business savvy to land a role in one of the industries that was hit hardest by 9/11. "If I'd allowed that dark cloud to smother me," she notes, "I never would have achieved my current position in the world, or my inner foundation of strength and confidence."

National events aren't the only type of wide-ranging adversities. A few years ago Irina Lunina, managing partner of Attollo Capital Partners, found herself in the midst of some serious upheaval in the financial services industry. She had arrived in the U.S. at the age of nineteen, and after earning a degree began working at Bear Stearns. She was well-regarded and within a short time was promoted into an institutional equity sales role. Her career was taking off.

One morning in early November of 2007, she began her day by chatting with colleagues and catching up on the details of their lives. Because of the amount of time they spent together, they felt like a family. Many had worked together for years. Then one of her coworkers was asked to visit the manager's office. Everyone knew something had gone terribly wrong. The coworker returned and started packing up his belongings. He'd been laid off. Unbelievably, more people from their group were called in. Each returned with a box and the same story.

"It was my turn," Lunina says. "I knew right away and was very calm. At the end, I think I just blocked my feelings because of the shock. We came in the office with the manager and the HR person said, 'I am sorry but your employment with Bear Stearns is terminated as of today. Do you have any questions?' I was numb."

It felt like her dream was over. She took a few months away from Wall Street and then started looking for opportunities. "Almost all my friends, coworkers, peers, clients were touched by this crisis and were seeking the way out," Lunina says. This, in part, helped spur her decision.

"I decided to open my own company since I knew that in these extraordinary circumstances I would be able to attract talent which would be impossible otherwise. Everybody was networking….everybody. I had called all my clients, peers and never once was turned away."

Attollo Capital Partners, LLC was born. The financial advisory firm focuses on Brazil, Russia, India and China (BRIC countries). Lunina and her employees recently celebrated their anniversary. Every year that celebration marks the time she faced bleak circumstances and turned her adversity into triumph.

On My Own

Like Irina, I took the entrepreneurial leap after changes shook my corporate career. When DuPont sold one of its underperforming divisions, the North Carolina offices were closed. I was asked to relocate but that wasn't a good option. At that time I was married and my husband was an entrepreneur with a stable income and I wasn't looking to make an uncertain move. So I took a severance package.

Before my end date, I began researching industries where my skills would be useful. I settled on promoting consumer brands to the public. I considered organizations that had brand-oriented roles or that placed a high value on marketing. I avoided companies in which the first budget to be cut during difficult times would be marketing. At one point, a radical new idea sparked. I was flipping through a magazine and really didn't feel like I was getting much out of it. So I began toying with the idea of putting together my own magazine. I jotted down thoughts about the types of articles it would include, cover stories and headlines, then shared the idea with a few friends.

When my time at DuPont ended, I continued trying to find a fulltime job. I interviewed for six months, talked with recruiters, hired resume reviewers, and participated in practice interviews but nothing worked. I wondered what I was doing wrong. One day one of my friends suggested I explore my vision for the magazine. I talked it over with my husband who thought it was something I would be great doing. Four months later I formed the company that would eventually become Diversity Woman Media.

In the early stages, I dealt with many of the challenges new business owners face, including a lack of capital. What I lacked in financial capital I more than made up for in social capital…in other words, I knew people and enjoyed meeting new people. My knowledge of the industry was limited, so I connected with people who were doing what I wanted to do. One of my acquaintances, Julie Milunic, owned an organic magazine that was doing really well. She was very helpful and made time in her schedule to meet with me and answer my questions. She mentored me on a range of publishing issues and helped me develop a sample magazine.

When potential advertisers saw the sample, I secured $16,000 in contracts within a week—enough for me to get a line of credit from the bank. Wow! I didn't stop there. I continued learning and discovered Stanford University's publishing program. I enrolled and gained valuable information along with a network of peers, distributors, printers, designers and other resources. I've built the business into the multimedia company you see today.

Starting a business from scratch is challenging, but so is taking over a family business. Sandra Westlund-Deenihan, president and design engineer of Quality Float Works, Inc., grew up in the manufacturing business founded by her grandfather. Although she had four sisters, she was the only one who took to the business. She earned an engineering degree, knew the suppliers, customers and employers, and learned how to close deals. When her father passed away, she was ready to take over.

But some people in the industry weren't quite ready for her. "I approached my new role with my chin up, ready to hit the ground running," Westlund-Deenihan says. "Instead, much to my surprise, I was not welcomed with open arms by the industry. I heard customers say repeatedly over the phone, 'Honey, can I speak to the owner of the company?' My heart sank."

Despite being well-qualified, she encountered adversity from those who didn't think a woman was up to the job. She endured condescending and insulting behavior from customers and suppliers. On one occasion, some people came in to see whether she had real equipment, employees and inventory. Her track record was solid—she was a third-generation manufacturing entrepreneur—but she was being treated like a startup.

Westlund-Deenihan didn't give up. Over the next few years her situation began to change. "I was surrounded by men in the industry so I played on their turf, by their rules," she says. "I used my skills and I beat them at their own game. I out-worked them, out-hustled them, out-performed and out-engineered them. I out-maneuvered them in every way. And, when times were hard, I took jobs no one else would do...a move that later proved key to the company's success."

Her company began making items other manufacturers shied away from. When conditions became favorable, her customers stuck with her and she cornered the market. Then changes in the industry spurred her to innovate and offer new products, which resulted in new opportunities in international markets. Perseverance paid off with respect, a profitable business, and exciting new business opportunities.

Turn Your Adversity into Opportunity

Nobody ever said the road to success is easy. Everyone faces obstacles; some personal, others professional, from minor and relatively trivial to major, life-changing events. Whatever the challenge, you can overcome it and make it work to your advantage. The following tips can help you stay sane and remain effective no matter what difficulties you are facing.

Stay Focused on Your Goal. When you're confronted by a challenge or are in the midst of difficult circumstances, it's easy to lose focus. This is especially true when the adversity is unexpected. You're already juggling career and family responsibilities or you might be starting a new business when suddenly you're confronted with a negative situation. Maybe you can't get funding for a new venture or that financial bonus you were expecting falls through. Someone might be spreading negative gossip that is impacting your career opportunities.

Don't think the challenge requires you to drop everything. Putting your current work on hold while you attempt to solve the new challenge is unlikely to be effective and might create additional difficulties. Instead, continue managing your various responsibilities and carve out some time to deal with the challenge. Prioritize the obstacle. If it's important enough to require immediate attention, develop a plan so you understand how much time will be required to manage the challenge. That can be built into your schedule more easily than a panicked response.

To figure out how to handle an obstacle, locate its root cause. If you're unable to secure funding, is the issue in your business plan or due to unfavorable economic conditions? Is the office gossip coming from colleagues who are jealous of your recent promotion or a former employee holding a grudge? In some cases, you might discover that the issue has more layers than you initially thought. Maybe the investors don't want to fund a woman-owned business. Perhaps the rumor mill hopes to demean you in order to discredit your supervisor.

Be prepared to deal with deeper and surprising issues that might surface. Above all, stay focused on your goals and follow your plan. Make adjustments as needed but continue to move forward in an informed, assured manner. However difficult the issue might seem, recognize that it's only temporary. When Lori Rosen, founder and CEO of The Rosen Group and managing partner of Blacksocks US, started her public relations firm, she maintained consistent growth. Her agency landed high-profile accounts like the New York International Automobile Show. But around the end of her fourth year, she was blindsided by her own employees.

"I returned to my office," Rosen says, "to find out that my account team was leaving to start their own firm, and taking the Auto Show account. I thought my business would suffer." But the loss of a lucrative account still had some positive benefits. "[I]t turns out," she says, "the account was a time strain for the office. We were devoting so many office resources to that account that other clients and prospects were neglected. All of our employees rallied together and ultimately, our business continued its growth spurt."

People she had invested in, paid and trusted did not reciprocate her loyalty. She turned her adversity into opportunity by strengthening the rest of her client relationships. Today the firm enjoys a highly regarded clientele list.

Eliminate External Distractions. It's hard to stay focused on your goals when you're facing criticism. While it's wise to look internally to determine how much of the challenge is your responsibility, be careful not to place all of the blame on yourself (something we women do all too often). Recognize that other forces are almost always at work. Unfortunately, when we face challenges others often criticize our conduct...and not in ways that are constructive.

Learn to compartmentalize criticism and address it when you're in the right frame of mind. Evaluate the motives of those who criticize you. Is it coming from a friend who is envious of your success or a family member who feels entitled to meddle in your child-rearing efforts? Or is it a mentor who genuinely wants you to succeed? Shield yourself from the negative commentary. Change the topic, end the conversation, do whatever is necessary to preserve your peace of mind. You don't have to listen to anyone's evaluation of your lifestyle. You are certainly not obligated to meet everyone's expectations!

Rely on Support. When you're facing adversity, it is essential that you support yourself. We often focus so much on the situation that we pay little attention to the impact on us personally. Offer yourself positive thoughts and words of encouragement. At the end of every day, think about your recent accomplishments. Remember that co-worker's quick question you answered to help her move forward. Consider the progress you've made on a client's venture or how your efforts will move your company forward. Use daily successes to remind yourself of your abilities and end your day on a positive note.

Use your network of friends, family and colleagues to lift your spirits. They can suggest different perspectives on events, share concerns and feelings, and bounce ideas around. Heather Ledeboer, owner of Mom 4 Life, found an incredible support network after she lost her baby at thirty-seven weeks. The gut-wrenching loss was compounded by the fact that she owned a boutique specializing in mom-invented baby products.

"I needed to decide how to proceed with my grief and pain without letting my business fall by the wayside," Ledeboer says. "I was blessed to have a staff that was not only understanding and supportive but also well trained and capable of stepping up to help take care of the day-to-day needs of the business."

She also focused on her own needs. "I began to blog about my journey of grief and what I was learning along the way," she says. "I discovered an amazing support being developed by my customers, and an opportunity to reach out to other moms who had lost babies was born. We emailed and shared and confirmed that our feelings were not crazy and we were not alone in our pain."

Own Your Own Power! In the midst of challenges, it's easy to feel helpless, stuck or inadequate. Don't allow yourself to sink under that burden. You always have some power, even when you don't feel like it. The trick is to figure out just what power you have and how you can use it to deal with whatever you're facing. Babz Barnett is the founder and president of Romp n' Roll Franchise Development, LLC. "One month before we opened our first Romp n' Roll location," Barnett says, "a major competitor (who had been in existence for many years) opened a franchise location a few miles away."

To make matters worse, her name shared that of the franchise! Rather than sit around and feel helpless, she figured out a way to distinguish her business from the competition. "Identifying how we were different," she says, "helped us clearly define who we were both to ourselves and to the public. [I]t helped us establish a mission statement and in turn strengthened our brand.... We put a major focus on providing superior customer service to everyone who walks through our doors which, I am proud to say, continues to be one of the many shining attributes of our company."

Keep Building Your Future. No matter what challenges you face, you must keep moving forward. Adversity happens and there is always a way through it to a new future. You cannot remain satisfied with the status quo and simultaneously build your future. Jenn Ormond, cofounder of Coffee Break Café, finally had enough.

"As a young student working my way through college as a bartender and waitress," Ormond says, "I relied on my customer service skills to earn a living. I was so tired of being treated terribly by counter help at local coffee shops, only to be served disgusting coffee. I was spending my hard-earned money to be treated poorly and drink something unworthy of drinking."

One day her future husband challenged her to stop complaining and do something about it. "We opened our first coffee shop," she says, "that focuses on excellent customer service and specialty coffee on March 3, 1996. I was twenty-five. He was twenty-seven." Recently the couple opened their fourth location. They feel that even if they get things wrong nine times, as entrepreneurs, they're always able to try number ten. That kind of attitude can build any future you envision!

The Opportunity of Adversity

Michele Hoskins, founder of Michele Foods Inc., turned a 150-year-old family recipe into a retail juggernaut. Before she opened the company, though, she had hit absolute bottom in her life. *Diversity Woman* featured her story in the summer 2013 edition as a way to showcase her story of triumph. She was in the middle of a divorce, had three young girls to support, was on welfare, and lived in the attic of her mother's home. This was clearly not the life she'd imagined for herself or her daughters. She wanted something more, and her daughters deserved a better start in life than what she was able to offer at the time. So she developed an old family recipe for breakfast syrup her great-grandmother had invented shortly after she'd been emancipated.

Her first test markets found that the syrup separated quickly and looked unappetizing until it was rewarmed. She applied for a program that would help bring her product to market in a professional manner while she perfected the formula. Her first contact with a buyer came only when she sat the entire day in a waiting room and was ushered into his office only after most of the employees had gone home.

That day and on all her other initial sales calls, everyone she spoke to was a white male. The process was intimidating. Eighteen years passed before she saw an African American buyer, and it took another few years before she met a female buyer. Even when she got in the door, she'd spend time after each visit researching the industry terms the buyers had used. "As a minority," Hoskins said, "I represented the consumers in this industry—we weren't taught how to become producers."

What Hoskins calls the Three Ps got her through. She had a passion that drove her forward through every adversity. Perseverance allowed her to rise to the challenges every day, no matter how difficult the road. Patience was her final virtue; by putting in her time, she built her own path brick by brick. Now the original Honey Crème Syrup and two other flavors anchor a multimillion-dollar business with products in more than 10,000 stores nationwide. She has turned her own adversity into opportunities for others through Michele's Mentoring Program, which has helped 150 entrepreneurs launch their own products.

In every life, storms will appear. Obstacles will fall across your path and criticism will arrive from unexpected quarters. In every case, look for the opportunity to grow. Expand your perspective so that you can see around the obstacle. Use the adversity to create new opportunities that serve your goals and desires. Be as innovative and creative in your problem-solving as you are when you're developing a new product or service. Dare to imagine a different life and you'll build a better, brighter future for yourself, your company and your employees.

CHAPTER TWO

Women and Power

POWER HAS BEEN CALLED the final frontier for women. The first women to venture into this new land in the corporate world found (or believed) that they had to look like men, talk like men, and manage like men. They had to watch what they said, censor their feelings, and weigh their every action against those of their male colleagues...because others were constantly judging the women's actions against those of men.

Then the light shone through. Strong communication skills, a naturally collaborative approach, and emotional intelligence were suddenly recognized as the keys to powerful leadership. While books and videos and workshops hustled to transform male leaders, women stepped up to the boardroom with these skills already firmly entrenched. They began to step into their power.

I define power as knowledge and wisdom. When you understand a situation fully and use the knowledge and wisdom you've gained from experience to resolve the issue, you're using your power. When you draw on your team or your peers to learn about new areas, you're gaining power. Every day, whether your projects run smoothly or fly off the rails, your efforts add to the wisdom that allows you to effectively execute your power.

The knowledge and wisdom I gained from my experiences are the reasons I launched *Diversity Woman* magazine, wrote this book, and founded the annual conference. During my time inside corporate America, I faced so many adversities…even more than the average person. In order to succeed, I had to use my knowledge and wisdom to create solutions. From an unsupportive supervisor who told me "you'll always be a secretary" to a long tenure at a Fortune 500 company to operating my own business, every step forward allowed me to become a more powerful woman.

As my power grew, so did my desire to support other women as they faced their own challenges. I wanted to teach them to overcome adversity with opportunity. I wanted them to recognize the power they held in their innate strengths and personal skills. By sharing my own experiences, I wanted them to learn that a positive attitude and an unrelenting focus on doing the right thing will see them through any crisis.

Giving back is also part of my power. Giving back prevents others from facing as many issues as I did. It helps them avoid the same trials, and when a certain situation can't be avoided, my efforts provide ready-made solutions. Problems can be eliminated through the simple equation of wisdom plus knowledge. When you add doing the right thing to that equation, your sum total equals power. The way you execute that power might be different than the methods men use…and the difference can have a substantial impact.

Stepping Into Your Power

Gail Becker, chair of the Global Women's Executive Network (GWEN) at Edelman, says, "Everyone has their own comfort level with exercising power. Many men are uncomfortable with it, and many women are not. But I do think that in general, women have a different way of exercising their power and different leadership styles from their male counterparts. Society is beginning to recognize and embrace these differences, and women are feeling more comfortable as power players in business."

Having women at the helm is good for everyone. More women should be in positions of power by operating their own businesses and commanding Fortune 1000 C-suites. The business world has already proven that having women in senior positions creates an excellent return on investment. Yet women don't always step into their power. The truth is that a dichotomy still exists between how men and women are viewed when they assert themselves the same way.

Soledad O'Brien, former host of *Starting Point* on CNN, was interviewed for *Diversity Woman* magazine's fall 2012 edition. During that interview, she said, "I grew up thinking that being aggressive was a positive thing." One day she was thrown off course during a meeting when a manager called her aggressive and "clearly meant it as something negative." The verbal attack brought her to tears after the meeting was over. She vowed to "never go to a meeting without an agenda. As a woman, it's important not to get sidetracked by someone." She never again let someone else's agenda deflect her from accessing her own power.

Her solution came from knowledge and wisdom. She learned that a powerful woman can be maligned for acting and speaking exactly as a male counterpart might. She applied her wisdom by ensuring that from then on she clearly communicated her agenda. Her aggressive pursuit of that agenda was then read as dedication to a specific goal. The issue was complex because it was (and still is) widespread. Her solution was simple and serves her to this day.

She pointed out that women should never be sidetracked by someone else's prejudices. That means we have to be aware of those beliefs. We all have to be aware of the fact that how we choose to wield our power might look very different than how people who came before us decided to wield their own. Our choices also might set us apart from our peers. Yet your way will probably be different, possibly very different, than the methods used by other women in power, even if they're in the same industry. Becker agrees when she says, "There is no one right way to lead or exude power, and I think women and society are beginning to embrace and celebrate that." As long as you respect your own values and honor your abilities, you will find the path to success for yourself and your company.

Exercising True Power

Edie Fraser, CEO of STEMconnector, says that a businesswoman's comfort level with using power at work depends on the corporate culture and the level she has achieved in that company. "In cultures that support innovation and diversity at their core, then yes [the woman is comfortable wielding power]. If the company is in a growth mode, yes as well. If there is the old-line, male chauvinistic culture, then [women proceed with] caution all the way."

Women will do best by placing themselves inside companies with cultures that work for them rather than against them. Management should be open to the power that comes from a strong work ethic and should value each individual's contributions regardless of their background, race or gender. Fraser recommends seeking out business leaders, male and female, who include other women "up, across and down the system."

Candice Reimer, senior program manager at Google, describes the different ways power is perceived. "Traditionally we think of power as being forceful, directive and dominant," she says. "I believe many women use more subtle forms of power. There is power in silence, and with active listening, one gains power. The most effective leaders in my work experience are those who focus on sharing power. They also flex different types of power according to the audience and the context."

Powerful Role Models

In early 2011, Gia Interlandi, former president of an educational and consulting firm called the Leadership Conservatory, wrote an article for *Diversity Woman* magazine. In the piece, titled "Share Your Vision," she stated that many female leaders are visionary. Despite this, they frequently keep their ideas to themselves. "Often they simply fail to recognize the power of their own vision or don't accept the responsibility to step up and speak their minds," she said.

She attributed these failings to a lack of role models. "While men have many role models to call on and are expected to share their vision, women have a much shorter list of accomplished public figures to call on as role models." I find role models all around me. The women featured in my magazine, those who speak at the conference and ones I network with daily inspire me with their own successful application of power.

Applying your power can happen at any age and any stage of your career. I knew a student who wanted to apply for an internship with the Terry Williams Agency, a highly influential public relations firm in New York City. The student thought that since she was from North Carolina, she would be considered too provincial for the position. Although she dearly wanted the job, she thought she had no hope. I told her to try. If she never even tried, she would never know how that company or others might respond.

I coached her as she wrote the letter of application. That short piece was the primary item that would be used to judge the different candidates, and I called on my knowledge and wisdom to help her create a letter they couldn't ignore. The entire time, she kept telling me that only two slots were open. I listened, allowing her to release those deep-seated fears while continuing to help with the letter. Her doubts disappeared the day the company called to say she had received one of the internships.

You probably think the story stops there. The student had reached for what she wanted, she'd utilized an experienced mentor's feedback, and she'd succeeded. Rather than celebrate, though, she called me back in tears. Her dreams were still out of reach because she couldn't afford to live in New York as a college student. A client of mine had recently purchased a brownstone, and a quick phone call determined that she was willing to rent out a room for the length of the internship. The student took the rental, accepted the position, and launched into the experience of her life!

Experiences like these prove that support for your vision doesn't have to come from the public domain, and sharing your vision doesn't require that you already be seated in a position of power. I was able to share a new vision for the student's life by assisting her one on one. Intimacy can be a powerful way to inspire others to follow their vision...and to inspire yourself. An important part of this begins within. If you hold a vision, you have to open yourself up and allow your own vision to sweep you away! Your passion and persistence—dare I say your aggressive pursuit of your goal?—will inspire your peers, your team and your boss. Sharing your vision is a prerequisite for successful leadership.

Role models truly are everywhere. Older, caring women who show courage in the face of poverty and cultural dislocation can inspire the next generation to greater heights. Mothers and fathers can cultivate and support the visionary adults their children will become. Other women who have established themselves as leaders in their industries can guide and encourage entrepreneurs. Since women relate to other women in business more easily than they relate to men, finding a mentor—or reaching out to mentor someone else—increases the opportunities for visionary women to rise.

"Visionary women are essential to society," Interlandi noted. "Through the hope and courage they spread, others find the voice to affirm their commitment to a grand idea and to each other."

Your career network is another area where you can step into your power. Build strategic alliances above, below, and in parallel with your position. With every new relationship, you broaden your perspective and identify new opportunities. That network also increases your visibility within the company. By applying the same steps outside your company, you'll expand your sphere of influence. Local business groups, volunteer activities, or even a sports team can create a journey of discovery with new friends and associates.

"The higher you move within your career, the more your network matters," said Marva Smith Battle-Bey, president of the Vermont Slauson Economic Development Corporation, in *Diversity Woman's* Nov/Dec 2008 edition. Remember that networks aren't all about you; they are also about who needs you and what you can offer them. "There is a quid pro quo in networking," Smith Battle-Bey pointed out, so build win-win alliances and create opportunities for cross-networking. Make introductions between people who can help each other, and ask for introductions to people you want to meet.

Lead with Power

The challenge with stepping into your power in a way that benefits you and others is that there is no blueprint for leadership. A variety of challenges confront leaders from CEOs to small business owners. Each challenge requires a different use of power. Being a powerful leader takes many forms, but at its root, a leader must arrive at work each and every day excited, positive, and ready to make a difference.

In our complex and rapidly evolving business world, excellent leadership requires thinking on your feet, confronting challenges, and having a game plan. One important component is to monitor your team for inappropriate or irresponsible use of power. Edie

Fraser says, "We are told to nip it early and stop bad behavior. There needs to be a warning and if not heeded, then this is not the right employee. [They aren't] the team player and builder one needs to succeed."

Roshni Phalgoo of Inspired Leaders Inc. knows how to handle inappropriate use of power. "When an employee wields power irresponsibly," she says, "it is time to start limiting that power. A great way to do this is through scheduled and frequent meetings where detailed objectives are laid out and powers limited and the execution of those objectives are discussed. Only those powers discussed each week can be executed, and the meetings will drive how that power is used."

Even if power is utilized appropriately, conflicts can arise at any point. Personalities clash, work styles don't mesh, or team members wrangle over who takes on certain tasks. Managing conflict is critical to powerful leadership. Heather Herndon Wright, senior director of affiliate relations at the Women's Business Enterprise National Council (WBENC), was interviewed for the Nov/Dec 2009 issue of *Diversity Woman*. She noted that when conflict arises, "it's time to sit down and talk about it. Deal with it head-on as early as possible. Conflict is like a festering wound. The longer it is there, the worse it festers."

The ways you'll handle each conflict will vary according to the situation. Developing an array of approaches will help, but one important aspect is being able to accept honest mistakes. Great leaders realize people aren't perfect. When your team takes a misstep, pinpoint the error, find a solution then move on. When you are the one who made the mistake admit it, figure out how to fix it, and move on. Dwelling on errors forces your entire team to drag deadweight that will only hold it back. Acknowledging that people are human beings frees them to take risks, innovate, and find the best path forward.

You of course must utilize your own power in positive ways. One is to delegate. Not only does handing off individual tasks make you more productive, it also turns you into a better leader. Catherine Crawley, founder of Crawley Communications & Research, wrote an extensive article on the topic for the Nov/Dec 2009 issue of *Diversity Woman*. Her research found that delegating allows others to develop their skills and expand their own network. When delegating is done well, employees feel engaged and empowered. Performance improves and productivity increases.

The biggest obstacle to delegating, Lisa Bing of Bing Consulting Group told Crawley, is the idea that if you want something done right, you must do it yourself. Some individuals fear that delegating will signal that they don't know how to perform a certain task. Asking for help might also be perceived as a sign of weakness. "It's a misguided perception that shared power reduces or diminishes one's power," Bing noted. "Sharing power actually expands one's sphere of influence."

Do be aware that cultural biases related to race, gender and ethnicity can snarl interactions. Anyone working in an industry dominated by men, for example, can find delegating particularly challenging. They might fear that male coworkers will think they aren't interested in the project or that they will come across as too demanding. Self-confidence is the key. Knowing that you have the ability to perform the task allows you to project the attitude of a leader: self-confident, powerful, and in control.

A few simple steps will help you delegate successfully. Be clear about the outcome required for each specific task. Identify the various elements that need to be addressed to achieve that outcome. Assign the task to the individual best qualified to handle the work, and define the milestones you will use to track that person's progress. With the right approach, faith in your own abilities and an understanding that no one can do it all alone, delegating becomes another tool with which to build success.

All these aspects of leadership (and more) can benefit from a mentor. It sounds counterintuitive, Crawley noted in her article, but great leaders need great mentors. Having women, particularly other African American women, in their networks has been positively tied to top promotion rates for women of that race. The same dynamic can benefit women regardless of their race, culture or background. Through mentors, leaders learn how to influence and inspire employees, respond to a challenge, build relationships, and create a corporate culture where people feel connected enough to move in the same direction.

Using Your Power for Others

Everything I do leverages my power to benefit others. I'm not alone in these efforts. Many of the women who have been featured in *Diversity Woman* magazine, who speak at the annual leadership conference and who were tapped for this book use their own knowledge and wisdom every day to benefit others. Edie Fraser, a woman who has been a fantastic mentor and advisor for my own career, offers some great advice on enhancing the power and strength of the people around us.

First, hand real responsibility to others. Clearly convey that they are responsible for their own performance. Those who can communicate in a compelling way should be given tasks oriented to their individual skills. Those who are able to build consensus and who can mentor others so they can also contribute are valuable parts of your team. Fraser finds that even generational differences in the workplace can be tapped in specific ways. "Include young people and use their entrepreneurial and technological genius to help you change and to exercise innovation, even disruptive innovation," she says.

In every case, people need to be allowed to make an impact. Part of creating success for yourself and your team comes from listening to the solutions, goals and dreams of every individual. Their success moves the project forward while enhancing their career options. "Then absorbing and praising their contributions is a natural consequence," Fraser concludes.

I've found that Fraser's points can have a real impact. The coaching sessions offered during the Diversity Woman Business Leadership Conference allows participants to engage in coaching sessions that help women recognize and honor their own capabilities. After the conference every year, I engage the coaches in a debriefing. We go through the issues attendees asked to address to ensure we are on track with our topics. Recently, the coaches reported that one of the top trends was a lack of confidence. Attendees struggled with their ability to respect their accomplishments and to honor the hard work they'd put into reaching career milestones. As a result, they found themselves faltering when they reached even further.

As women, we sometimes believe that any little blemish will be held against us. We obsess over whether our clothes are too masculine or too sensual. We parse every word we've spoken to our superiors and examine every piece of guidance we pass along to our teams. Sometimes being the only woman in the room feels so intimidating we don't speak up as often as we could...or even as often as we should. The conference provides wisdom, knowledge, and solutions for these types of issues. Belief in yourself and your ideas makes you a leader even when you're nowhere near the boardroom.

The same innovative dynamic Fraser pinpointed as being so effective inside an organization can be equally effective outside the corporate walls. When Danae Ringelmann was with J.P. Morgan, she told *Diversity Woman* magazine in the Nov/Dec 2009 edition, she attended a Hollywood-meets-Wall Street event. Since her badge identified her as a financial analyst, she said, "People thought I was there to finance films. I remember clearly an accomplished seventy-year-old filmmaker who was begging me for money."

At the time, Ringlemann was twenty-two years old. She felt heartbroken that so many talented individuals lacked the funding necessary to bring their dreams to life. She knew there had to be a better way. She spent years studying the business models of entertainment companies like Dreamworks and Pixar. By 2008, she and her two colleagues announced their new company, Indiegogo, an online social marketplace that helps filmmakers solicit funding from fans. Within a year, some 800 films had been posted to the site and 15 projects had raised more than $70,000 each.

Today the site includes all industries. As the leading international crowdfunding platform, Indiegogo has raised millions of dollars for thousands of campaigns. In providing filmmakers with more choices and the power to fund their own projects, Ringlemann aligned her values with her career. Not only did she build a company and a career she loves, she's helping others build the same things in their lives. Her story and all the others I've shared in this chapter prove that women are advancing into high-level positions at a rapid rate. We are becoming confident, effective leaders without compromising our personal values or style.

Your Position of Power

Belief in myself—my abilities, my skills, and the value of my goals—marks every area of my life. My personal quest includes boosting my own leadership skills, of course, along with goals and game plans that will shape my personal and professional future. In 2011, I earned a Master's in Entrepreneurship, was inducted into Beta Gamma Sigma National Honor Society, and was chosen by my graduate school's College of Business faculty as Most Outstanding Student. I was also honored to be named 2011 Minority Business Person of the Year by my local Chamber of Commerce. At the end of 2015, I will receive an Education Doctorate in Leadership.

Why do I push myself so hard? To help myself and to enable myself to help others. In order to compete in today's ever-changing world, we must constantly innovate and reinvent our businesses and ourselves. I actually relish the opportunity to grow. Learning new things is always empowering. And I am quick to pass on that information through the many channels of communication I've built with Diversity Woman Media so others can navigate the competitive business landscape and advance to new heights.

The equation for power is simple. Knowledge plus wisdom creates benefits for your own career and life. Approach each situation with the desire to learn everything you can about that situation. Utilize your team members, peers, mentors and sponsors to add to your understanding. Then draw on your experience to find the wisdom to resolve situations in a positive way. When you share your knowledge and wisdom with other women, you'll help them develop their own power. Step up. Step out. Step into your power!

CHAPTER THREE

Myth Busters

AS LEADERS ENSURE THAT MORE women are placed in positions where they can develop their talents right from the start, more female employees will rise into managerial positions. The leadership skills they employ in midlevel positions qualify them to step into the C-suite. Over time the numbers tilt in favor of balanced power, increased innovation, and enhanced profitability. To encourage employees along this pathway, the work environment must be safe.

Katherine Giscombe is the vice president of Global Member Services for Catalyst, which provides research and advice about women at work. She appeared in *Diversity Woman*'s Point of View column in fall of 2013. She stated that the ability to share information, opinions and personal anecdotes connects managers and employees while it builds peer-to-peer networks. But for women, negative stereotypes and the greater scrutiny of "outsiders" (men, any individual not from the same ethnic or cultural background, etc.) means that sharing can make women feel vulnerable.

One African American woman told Giscombe about a period during which she experienced car trouble. A male colleague said, "You're always having problems with your car." The comment felt so judgmental the woman decided to never again share her personal business at work. Guarding against myths can interfere with professional relationships. While sharing can involve risk, cultivating the trust that goes hand in hand with sharing is critical. Trust makes it easier to discover solutions to workplace issues and to connect on projects that require teamwork.

Giscombe recommended offering personal information that relates to the workplace. A woman might talk about her role with a community nonprofit, for example, to highlight her ability to take charge, lead individuals from many backgrounds, and achieve goals. My approach to breaking any myth is all about empowering the individual woman. When you encounter myths and stereotypes, remember that how you take charge of your career is entirely up to you. Anyone can promote themselves during a performance review or opt into a job that requires seventy-hour work weeks and months away from the family every year. Rather than allowing others to define what your career should look like, true diversity and inclusion results from defining your own style.

You can be a successful leader even if you allow a team member to telecommute a few days a week so she can care for her ailing mother. You can be a successful leader without raising your voice. You don't have to have a prototypical male style to speed yourself along your trajectory. Success in the workplace, as in other parts of life, means being yourself. When we are all able to be our true selves, we achieve the highest form of diversity.

Destroying Myths

In all my years running Diversity Woman Media, I've met plenty of people who are shattering myths about women in the workplace.

If I had to select one woman to exemplify the passion, persistence, determination and business savvy of a true myth buster, she would be Lynn Tilton. She was a keynote speaker at the 2012 leadership conference and was featured on the cover of *Diversity Woman*'s fall 2013 magazine. During her lifetime, Tilton has broken many myths—her appearance is often commented on in national media, she is a self-made financial success, she possesses the intellect required in a turnaround CEO, she cultivates and maintains a broad vision, and she is known for her tough management style.

Since 2000 Tilton's private equity company, Patriarch Partners, has bought and restructured over 150 distressed manufacturing companies. Today it manages 75 companies in 14 industries and rakes in revenues topping $8 billion. Her portfolio constitutes the largest woman-owned business in the U.S. Hard work and dedication have made Tilton one of only a handful of self-made female billionaires in the nation.

Despite her drive, her success and her ongoing mission to revive the American manufacturing base, the media tends more often than not to focus on her style...and yes, that means mostly her clothes. Leather and stilettos accessorized with salty language make her one of the most polarizing CEOs in our country today. Her methods are also considered somewhat controversial. Tilton feels that the criticisms are largely a function of a male-dominated financial industry that can't handle a successful woman who does things her way.

"If I were a man," she said of her tough management style, "I would be seen as rose petals softly falling from the heavens. When we don't do what we need to do, companies fail and people get hurt. I need people who work for me to understand that [my style] is not about them. I need people who are mission oriented."

I wholeheartedly agree. Many people are still laboring under the misconception that to make it into the C-suite or to be successful in general a woman has to be "the b-word." My leadership style has a softer approach. The driving force behind it is a desire to create a win-win situation for everyone involved in any project or plan. However, that doesn't mean I can't learn from another woman's very different leadership methods. When a situation requires a more direct approach, I can just as easily pluck something from a more direct leadership style and utilize it to achieve a successful outcome.

As women, it's important that we never judge another woman's leadership style. In an ideal world, I would be able to easily negotiate every situation with an open heart and a gentle hand. In the real world, we all have to adjust course sometimes. The time I've spent with Tilton has been a fantastic opportunity to see firsthand how another person's very different leadership style can generate top-tier results. My admiration and respect for her as a woman, as a leader, and as a professional businesswoman has no limit. The things I learned from her have enhanced my personal style of leadership.

Once you open yourself to learning from others, you'll find plenty of opportunities. While talking with Tilton I discovered that, like me, her background had a strong impact on her career. A child of immigrants, she reached far above her position and attended Yale. Soon she was a single mother working 100 hours a week on Wall Street. A change was in order, one that would allow her to do nothing less than save American manufacturing.

Using the $10 million she'd saved, she founded Patriarch Partners. In her role as a turnaround CEO, Tilton rebuilds iconic American brands like Rand McNally, Spiegel catalog, Stila Cosmetics and MD Helicopters. Tilton loves what she does. She is unapologetic about her public persona as a provocative, ball-busting billionaire. The hot-pink lipstick and leather, or at least the attention it commands, is a strategic advantage. Her carefully cultivated persona demonstrates that women do not have to follow a specific template to succeed in a male-dominated industry.

"In general," she said, "when women change who they are and try to be other than who they are, their chances of success are exponentially diminished. I have taken it to an extreme because I want other women to see that they don't have to change who they are. You can be bright and sparkly and beautiful or smart and sexy and sophisticated and still take on male-dominated industries and win. What I wear and how I look are making a point. It's like the four-minute mile: when someone finally does it, you know it's possible."

Judy Tomlinson, founder and chief creative officer of two different companies, faces myths in the world of technology. AvocSoft develops mobile applications while FashionTEQ creates wearable technology, combining high-tech functions with high fashion. The top myth women have to face in her industry, she says, is that they lack the intellect and ability to excel. "Women are just as smart as men," she notes, "and as capable."

Within the categories of science, technology, engineering and mathematics (known as STEM), gender-based myths are taking longer to break, partly because of exposure. While many people would agree that no industry is better suited to a specific gender, America isn't doing a great job introducing girls (or boys) to professions that cross traditional gender lines. Girls Who Code, a non-profit that lobbies for computer science classes in public schools, lists forensic science and medicine as their young members' most popular career choices. It's not that girls are especially drawn to law enforcement or medical careers; instead, they see those jobs displayed on dozens of popular TV shows and movies. They gravitate toward what they've been exposed to.

Ada Lovelace, called the "enchantress of numbers," wrote the first computer program in 1842, so all the myths about women and girls lacking a natural talent for industries like science and technology were never true. Still, Tomlinson notes that she doesn't see enough women in her industry. "If they are there," she says, "they are not as recognized as men" because men are often selected to lead important projects. Despite having held positions at a number of engineering companies, "Rarely do I see a woman in charge of technical projects. I have always worked for a man in charge of the project and the team. Maybe there is somewhat of a change now but I don't think much."

Diversity Woman Media has been a leader in acknowledging women in the STEM field and shining a spotlight on their achievements. The magazine has covered entrepreneurs who launched their own apps and social media sites to CEOs in STEM industries. The more women and girls see their own faces staring back at them from all levels of the corporate and business worlds, the greater their confidence will be to enter these fields and make a real difference in their lives and for their companies.

Subtle and Self-generated Myths

Advances in civil rights and recognition of how women can contribute to the bottom line have helped destroy some of the more ridiculous myths about women in business. Any overt support that still remains has for the most part been banished from the boardroom and the manufacturing floor. But subtle myths and the equally subtle ways those myths function can still sabotage a career. And because certain myths lingered for so long, women might harbor those myths in their minds. Only by examining them up close can we eliminate each and every one.

Vera Moore is a perfect example of how a woman's different perspective can capitalize on new opportunities while offering more than monetary rewards. *Diversity Woman* magazine featured her in the fall 2013 edition. As president and CEO of Vera Moore Cosmetics, she works under the premise that entrepreneurial success is about more than financial gain. Her story began while she was working on *Another World,* a televised soap opera that ran for thirty-five years. Back in the early 1970s, makeup wasn't tailored to the ethnic market, especially people of a darker hue. Moore moved immediately to fill the void.

Just as she had found in the acting world, the business world sent a lot of rejections her way. Through persistence, she built a cosmetic empire. The company's products are now used on stage, screen and television shows. Along the way, she's fulfilled her mission to touch her customers in a deeper way. "It's important for me to empower women," Moore said, "even with the cosmetics. It just felt good to me that I would empower them. So this entrepreneurship thing was not only about [my own] economic empowerment. It was about [my customers'] self-esteem."

Her background makes her every word ring with conviction. She was the first African American soap opera actress. She launched a company to serve and empower an underrepresented market. And through it all, she has kept Moore Cosmetics a family-owned business. She even offers a line of skincare products for men. The secret behind her ability to bust through so many myths is simple: stay focused on who you are and what you have to offer.

"There's always a ceiling," she said, "but so what? If I worried about that, I would have said, 'I can't do that. I'm black.' I don't even deal with that. If you are born black, you're going to die black—get over it. You have to hone your skills so when you walk in that door, no matter where you are, you're walking in as a professional person. It's the same with the old boy network. You can't worry about that either. You keep your eyes on the prize."

While Moore took her family-owned business worldwide, I faced a different kind of upheaval in my household when I found myself divorced after fourteen years of marriage. I had heard that wives end up ten times worse financially after separating from a spouse, while husbands end up ten times stronger financially. Through hard work and a belief in my own abilities, how I handled my divorce turned out to be one of the greatest successes of my life!

Another myth that haunts women is that divorce is a sign of failure. This is actually the worst story we can believe because some people will stay in a bad situation for fear that they will be considered a failure. It takes insight and a great deal of honesty to recognize you are not compatible with your partner. Courage and self-respect are required for a woman to make the decision to resolve the issue. The same thing happens in the workplace and in business. What you do with this realization proves true success and not failure.

As soon as it became clear that the marriage was over, I led every part of the proceedings by example. I treated the divorce like a business transaction. I maintained dignity and respect for everyone involved. That doesn't mean there weren't tough times or that the reasons the marriage ended weren't upsetting. No matter what happened, I never let my frustration or disappointment or pain show. Regardless of what was said to me or about me or who said it, I maintained a calm, balanced approach.

My ex's needs and goals were no longer my concern. If the fastest and easiest solution was to let things go—property, hurt feelings, old grudges and all—then that's what I did. Today my ex and I are amicably co-parenting our sixteen year old. I came out ahead because I focused on what was right. I didn't allow my feelings to drive my actions. Throughout the process, I turned my attention to my needs and those of my daughter.

To that end, I laid out a plan for this life transition. I sketched out a one-year, three-year and five-year plan. Before the divorce was finalized, I had received my master's degree and changed my company's business model. I didn't swerve into my ex's lane and allow myself to get off track. I stayed in my own lane and stayed focused on myself. Because I led by example, I ended up ten times better off. The same approach served me when DuPont laid me off. Where was I supposed to go after a fourteen-year career with a top-tier company? Anything else seemed anticlimactic…at first. By stepping back and considering what I could do to better myself and my position, I ended up better off than before.

The woman I am today personally and professionally is due in part to my divorce. While writing this book, I became a candidate for a doctorate. Now *Diversity Woman* magazine is carried on the newsstands of Barnes & Noble stores across the nation, my Twitter feed is trending #1 in diversity, and the annual conference has been recognized as the #1 business leadership conference for diverse and multicultural women. Every year, testimony pours in about how the conference workshops and presentations support and transform attendees' lives.

Like Moore, I achieved economic success as I pursued my true goal. Although financial stability is important, the personal success has been much more profound. The divorce allowed me to empower myself in new ways. Every challenge presented an opportunity to grow, to step into new power, and to prove through example that other women can achieve the same. By busting the divorce myth, I have carved a pathway for others to follow to their own success whether they divorce, choose to never marry, or remain single for long periods.

Break Out of the Traditional Box

As for career fields that have been traditionally viewed as "men's work," barriers for women are constantly breaking down or have already been removed. Megan Sage has spent a lifetime involved in the military, electronics and aviation fields. Although women enter these fields in lower numbers than men, Sage says the barrier to entry has nothing to do with being female. Instead people must prove themselves to be trustworthy contributors who understand that they are supporting a warfighter.

"The myth that it's easier for men to enter these fields and succeed is untrue," she says. "It is a tough industry period. I didn't have anyone telling me I couldn't be in this industry because I was a woman, but I had people telling me that it is hard to be successful in this industry as a start-up manufacturer. I will agree that's true!"

Her experience in the aerospace and defense industry began when she was thirty-one. She owned a radio frequency/microwave precision electronics components manufacturing company. Although Sage couldn't locate role models (male or female), that didn't present a problem. "I had bigger issues like getting business for my company," she says, "especially when I recognized the technical superiority of our products."

She notes, however, that the military's culture still harbors threads of old ideas about women. When she interviewed an apache pilot on power and politics, she asked how women fared in his world. He said, "Great, no problem!" Her follow-up question was, "OK then how many woman are in your command?" The answer was none.

Women are just beginning to deeply experience careers through military enrollment, employment as government civilians, and supply or service contractors. "It truly is a good old boy network and on top of that, science and engineering is still predominantly male," Sage notes. "So the perceived myth that it is harder for woman is very culturally real just by the nature of the work. That is just the nature and heritage of our military in the United States."

She faced the challenge with the persistence and determination every woman needs. "I chased the technical challenges and armed myself with data," she says. "I went out to represent my company in the Army electronics and aviation community and had to figure it out on my own. I learned by observation of protocol and took every opportunity to attend industry conferences and symposiums to not only meet people but more importantly to learn the electronics systems and platforms and how they were used."

While attending the technical conferences and program industry briefings, she was able to seek out new contacts and reach out to potential clients. Out of hundreds of attendees, perhaps ten would be women. Of those ten, half would be managing the details of registration, meals, check-in, and the like. The other five would be in the audience with her. That was the mid-2000s. Today things are slowly changing. "Maybe in the physics and RF/microwave lectures there are now ten women sitting," she notes of more recent conferences. "I also found in the software and IT world about a quarter of conference attendees are women."

Although change arrives more slowly in the military, Sage notes that a woman CEO stands at the helm of one of the top U.S. contractors, a woman leads the electronics division of another, several notable woman hold leadership roles at Army Material Command, and the first leader of the Army Electronic Warfare Proponent Office was a woman. These women and others are pioneers who have, she notes, "most certainly paid their dues."

So has Sage. Last summer, she went to dinner with four old friends who were longtime Army consultants and retired Army service personnel. She had competed against some of them, and had engaged one in a head-to-head battle for work...that she won, by the way! One of the men at the table had met her only recently. As he discussed a program and began offering his opinion, he hesitated. Sage's competitor told him, "It's OK. Megan is one of the guys."

That was a great compliment. Being one of the guys meant she was trusted and was considered a warrior in it for the long haul. "I have had the boots on the ground by showing and participating in this world," she says. "I spend the time to get to know people with genuine interest. That goes a long way in a tight network of players."

Like most other industries, the aerospace and defense arena is very much driven by relationships and values. Women who deliver and who can support an intricate network of relationships will succeed. Sage has discovered proof of this time and again, most recently when she attended an IT USAF conference in D.C. There she met up with a friend who'd become a one-star general. "I was so happy for him," she says. "He is a very smart guy, dedicated to our nation and also very kind to people. He evokes leadership in others through the way he listens to people and gives them time."

The general was so excited to see her again he insisted she sit with him and five other active generals at the head table. Rather than ask business questions, she enjoyed the opportunity to get to know them as people. At the end of the day she really thanked her friend and told him how wonderful it had been to meet the other generals. He said, "Megan, it is not who you know, it is who knows who you are."

Sage accomplished her success through a true love for her work, her passion for technology, and by being authentic. Those qualities are appreciated by everyone she has contact with. Remember her efforts and apply her approach to your own work. Lead by example and you'll lead yourself forward in every industry.

And while you're building your career, know that your reach is unlimited. In *Diversity Woman*'s Point of View column for the winter 2011 edition, Stedman Graham, founder of S. Graham & Associates, tackled the myth that women should only aspire to a certain level of success. The author of *Identity: Your Passport to Success* feels that identity has a profound influence on how successful women are in the corporate world. Far too many people labor under the influence of subtle myths that can limit the future they envision for themselves. These myths generate internally because women and people of color aren't always taught to maximize their potential.

"They are often led to believe that they should only aspire to reach a certain level," Graham said. "They're not supposed to be part of the American free enterprise system or the global marketplace." These messages are often passed down from generation to generation. Messages received from families are often reinforced by the outside world. Belief in the myths influences behavior, and suddenly individuals have placed limits on themselves.

As an African American man, Graham speaks from experience. For a long time, he lived in a box imposed by generational messages. Like many people, he allowed others to decide who he was and who he could become. Then one day he set himself free. "I discovered how powerful knowledge is," he said. "That helped me break through a lot of the barriers and focus on my core values—and who I really am—and I found my passion."

If you can break out of the box, there's nothing you can't accomplish. Once you've stripped away those self-limiting labels, you can create a career based on your unique talents, skills and identity. You can remain underutilized at work and unrecognized for your true abilities or you can bust free and take ownership of your life. "The most authentic thing a woman can do is be who she is," Graham noted, "and never apologize for who she is."

I couldn't say it better myself.

Myths of Gender Dynamics

Women and men hold common misconceptions about how women approach business…that they are less interested in the bottom line, for example, or that they are less effective because they have a "softer" approach. While men and women certainly have basic differences, who's at the helm doesn't really matter. The truth is that no company's approach is exactly the same as another's because each leader brings her own ideas, concepts and visions into play. By being aware of the myths involved in gender dynamics, we empower ourselves and the women around us to break free.

Sherri Goodman, senior vice president and general counsel for CNA, is also in the military security and defense arena. Her non-profit research organization operates the Center for Naval Analyses and the Institute for Public Research. In her industry, the top myth women must confront is that they aren't as tough as men. "Women have not had full ability to participate in combat historically," she notes. "Women were not seen as warriors. But that myth was fully busted in the Iraq and Afghanistan wars."

Women also now serve as CEOs of major defense contractors like BAE, Lockheed and General Dynamics. America has also had female Secretaries of State and in the role of National Security Advisor. Goodman predicts that soon the U.S. will have a female Secretary of Defense. Before her tenure with CNA, she served nearly a decade as Deputy Undersecretary of Defense as the Pentagon's chief environmental, safety and occupational health officer. Even though she was one of the highest-ranking women to serve the DOD, she started in 1993, a time when some people weren't willing to take women seriously.

Her approach was simple. She called on her personal wellspring of persistence. She continued to push for what she believe reflected right values for the military mission such as the full integration of women and minorities, environmental protection, and care for military families. Even though it took a while, in the end, she notes, the U.S. military always moves in the right direction. The changes she and thousands of other hardworking people were able to achieve made the military more inclusive, dynamic, and innovative than ever before.

The private sector had its own ossified myths to overcome. Jeffery Tobias Halter, who bills himself as the leading male expert in helping organizations value women, has a deep understanding of gender dynamics in the workplace. As president of YWomen, he brings thirty years of experience with top companies to promoting the significant role women can play. Halter believes that one huge myth standing in women's way is that hard work and outstanding results will be enough to move forward.

He points out that in a study by the Hidden Brain Drain Task Force, 77% of women believe promotions were driven by a combination of hard work, long hours, and educational credentials. By comparison, 83% of men readily acknowledged that who you know counts for at least as much as job performance.

"At the top levels of an organization," Halter notes, "outstanding results are a given...they're part of a baseline of expectation. So the real differentiators that will help you move ahead are others' perceptions of you (positive, negative or unknown), whether you have a breadth of experience and exposure, and whether others are willing to go to bat for you."

The myth that performance trumps all presents a double whammy. Not only do women rely on hard work alone to get ahead, they also fail to utilize advocates and sponsors who can support their advancement. "Women's networks are much broader than men's," Halter points out, "but women are often hesitant to use their network for personal gain. Men have no issue doing this."

Over the course of several years, Halter mentored a young woman. "She was absolutely the hardest working person I have ever known," he explains. "Her work was impeccable and the results outstanding." But she operated in the field in Michigan for a company headquartered in Atlanta. The scattered geography offered few opportunities for face-to-face meetings with influential people. At the same time, her manager did very little to talk up any of his employees, including her.

The company held quarterly meetings at their regional office in Chicago and an annual meeting at their Atlanta headquarters. Each year the young woman arrived just in time for the meeting and left immediately afterward. She never added a day on either side to meet with the other regional sales people who were her peers.

Even during breaks at the meetings, she never wasted a moment chitchatting and instead spent every minute on her phone working. Despite Halter's constant coaching, the woman continued to believe that performance would lift her up the corporate ladder.

At some point, she finally paused long enough to look around. She realized that a majority of her peers, whose results were comparable but certainly not better than hers, had made vice president. Only then did she start to believe Halter's advice. "This woman could have been a VP almost five years earlier if she had been much more mindful about building relationships," Halter says. "I not only believe she lost out but I think the company lost out by not promoting her sooner."

Don't lose out because you're following the rules of some mythological holdover from the old boys network. Eliminate the subtle myths that have embedded themselves in your thoughts. Grab for everything you're worth. And you are worth it. Even if you don't know that yet, I do!

Flip the Myth

Whether you're a man or a woman, if you're reading this book, you already know that this chapter has touched on only a few of the myths that face women of every race, culture and background. We've looked at how they can present obstacles and lead you down paths that won't go anywhere near your goals. Now I invite you to truly step into your power by using those same myths to generate success, inspiration, creativity, passion, happiness and authenticity in your career and your life.

Farnaz Wallace of Farnaz Global had to do this as an Iranian-American woman working her way up in a U.S. company. She admits that she was a far cry from the traditional stereotype of a businessman...not just in her appearance but also in her professional approach and her leadership style. "So of course there were obstacles," she says, "but I overcame those obstacles by generating results and gaining trust and respect."

Remember that this was a time when women were being told by all the experts (notably male experts) that to get ahead, they had to look, think, act and talk like men. Utilizing her own methods and approaches set Wallace even further apart from her peers than her background, her culture or her gender. She turned in a powerhouse performance, of course...and she made sure the people around her knew who she was and what she was capable of doing. Taken together, these achievements allowed her to lay each stepping stone in her own career path.

The biggest obstacle reared up in the same area so many other women struggle to conquer: contract terms and compensation negotiations. "I was paid less than my executive counterparts not just because I was a woman," she explains, "but because they could get away with it due to my own lack of negotiation skills. Once I learned those skills and gained confidence, those barriers were removed."

Although the vestiges of gender-based myths still have a tenuous hold in some companies, Wallace doesn't think women have to fight as hard today. "A lot has changed," she says of corporate America, "and will continue changing. That's just part of the natural course of evolution. With 25% of baby boomers retiring by 2016, I think the workplace will look and feel very different. Gen Xers already have displayed major cultural shifts in gender roles, and we continue experiencing an even bigger shift with Gen Y."

Still, certain challenges hang on. In particular, Wallace notes, "The question remains unanswered whether women want the top corporate positions. A lot of research points to the fact that, for a variety of reasons, they don't." If you're unfamiliar with that research, it boils down to work/life balance, concerns that being ambitious is a negative trait, and that the stress and other negative health effects are too high a price. Steve Reinemund, who was interviewed for the winter 2013 issue of *Diversity Woman*, might have part of the answer.

Formerly chairman and CEO of PepsiCo, Reinemund is now dean of Wake Forest University Schools of Business. Rather than blame the deep doubts women supposedly suffer over work/family conflicts, he pinpoints earlier events in women's lives that have nothing to do with their personalities or their goals. "The pipeline positions for women on track to C-suite roles starts to narrow even before business school," he noted.

He has found that educational institutions are themselves remiss in developing women in a way that enhances their opportunities later in life, particularly in terms of preparing them for executive career tracks. Statistics bear out his claim. In 2010, less than a third of applicants to fulltime MBA programs were female. "Educators and corporate leaders have a duty to develop future leaders," he said. "Because men are currently in the majority of corporate leadership positions, we have the opportunity to sponsor and mentor women and help change the landscape in corporate boardrooms."

To that end, Wake Forest created a Master of Arts in Management to immerse liberal arts, science, and engineering grads in business concepts. The program has consistently attracted a higher percentage of women and underrepresented groups than MBA programs. By turning away from the distracting debate over which gender feels more pressure to provide childcare and complete household chores, he's found a concrete and realistic way to clear the path to the C-suite. He is flipping a myth on its head by locating one of the real reasons women are waylaid in their careers.

Andra Rush of Rush Trucking flipped the myth that women in male-dominated industries aren't given the chance to prove themselves. Her accomplishments were so impressive she was on the cover of *Diversity Woman* in Nov/Dec of 2008. As she built her business from the ground up, she found that raising eyebrows in the male-dominated industry garnered more attention for her company. When she delivered on service contracts no one else would touch, she not only proved herself capable, she garnered client loyalty and contracts that allowed her to expand into a national presence.

After starting out in nursing, her father's advice about working for herself came back to her. He'd always told her it was the only way to really get ahead. And having seen the poverty in the Mohawk nation and other First Nations tribes, she knew that owning her own company was the way to go. When Rush Trucking Corporation launched in Detroit in 1984, the female founder started busting myths from day one. She helped her fledgling team with everything from oil changes to mechanics. On days when the company had more runs than drivers, she made deliveries herself.

Beginning with a fleet numbering a mere two trucks, Rush grew her company into a multimillion-dollar enterprise. Her 920 drivers now transport everything from auto parts to potato chips throughout the continental U.S. and Canada with interlines in Mexico. The fleet is a little larger now with 900 tractors and 1,800 trailers. Proving that she could succeed in a male-dominated industry was part of the appeal.

As a woman in that industry, especially one who was in control of the business, she raised eyebrows. She believes it got her jobs she might otherwise never have received...a sort of "Let's see what she can do" dynamic. Time and again, she surprised her clients pleasantly. Because of the myth, many of her initial clients hadn't listed her as their first choice. They called only after none of the other companies could meet their delivery deadlines.

"When you bail someone out of a jam," she noted, "you get moved to the top of the list." She also believes being a woman pushed her to greater heights. Even when customers' expectations were lofty, she met and exceeded them. She took tough routes... and knew when to say no to jobs that weren't a good fit. Her entrepreneurial spirit and willingness to tackle new challenges served the company well in other ways. Rush innovated by being one of the first trucking companies in the region to track freight using satellite technology.

Today she continues helping others pave their own roads to success. She has created a positive work culture that enables employees to feel they become better people by working there. By coaching women- and minority-owned businesses who lose bids, she pays it forward by helping them do better next time. Rush used a myth in a male-dominated industry to her company's benefit... and shattered the myth forever.

Flipping myths on their heads turns adversity into opportunity. The willingness to face this kind of challenge is one of the core components of leadership. No matter what your race, culture or background, naysayers will always try to mislead you, devalue your worth, and tear down what you build. Anyone who takes those myths to heart allows others to control their destinies. Perseverance and determination along with a healthy belief in your abilities will shatter any myth you encounter. Move forward every day. Shrug off the myths or flip them so they benefit you and your business. That is the best kind of example from the best kind of leader.

The End of the Tale

A variety of myths present obstacles for women in the workplace. Some of the women spotlighted here used those myths as motivation...they decided that busting the myth added an extra dimension to the work they were doing and charged forward in ways that shattered the old stereotypes. Others flipped the myths and rewrote the old tropes into stories of success. You might not be able to avoid myths entirely, not until our world finally advances enough to truly honor and respect individuals from every race, culture and background. With determination, self-confidence and wisdom, you can bust any myth you do encounter. You can achieve full and abundant success in your career and your life!

CHAPTER FOUR

Inclusion is Good Business

I CAN STATE UNEQUIVOCALLY that the heart of inclusion is the heart of every human being. In late 2010, I was privileged to host Dr. Maya Angelou at Diversity Woman Media's annual leadership conference. During the conference, we presented her with our Mosaic Woman Legend Award. The award recognizes a woman whose accomplishments, inspiration and brilliance have impacted the lives and careers of women of all races, cultures and backgrounds. As Dr. Angelou spoke, she addressed "the African-American, White-American, Asian-American, Spanish-American, fat-American, pretty-, plain-, gay-, and straight-American" audience.

Those words capture my mission exactly. When a company or even a department has calcified to the point that qualified individuals are turned away based on judgments that have nothing to do with performance, its downward slide has already begun. Although great advances have been made in eliminating discrimination of all types, more work needs to be done. Companies today are also being challenged by the need to become good global citizens that welcome individuals from other places...and that are themselves welcomed into other nations.

The pallet offered by people of color, those who are visibly or invisibly disabled, members of the LGBT community, people of different ages, and those from different religious or spiritual backgrounds expands a company's ability to face new challenges and innovate based on different perspectives. By employing people who represent the entire range of human beings, businesses of every size can access some of the fastest-growing markets in the United States. Inclusion is not just the right thing to do. Inclusion is good business.

Inclusion Provides a Strong ROI

Jackie Glenn, Vice President and Chief Diversity Officer of the world's leading information infrastructure technology and solutions company, appeared in the fall 2011 edition of *Diversity Woman*. Glenn knows that inclusion is about return on investment. "Since we're in technology," she said of EMC, "innovation is our lifeblood, and to achieve the highest levels of innovation, you need diversity. You simply can't have the same types of people at the table making decisions. Numerous studies have shown that having different perspectives is more powerful in driving the emergence of new ideas, making more accurate predictions, and coming up with more effective problem-solving than the traditional likeminded group...."

In fact, studies show that when members of a minority group are present, members of the majority group make a greater effort. Having women on a board might promote stronger performance from its male members. Employees from different racial and cultural backgrounds can push white American coworkers to achieve more. Individuals from the LGBT community, those who are disabled, are from different religious backgrounds and plus-size people energize employees from outside their affinity group to reach farther, drive harder, and achieve more.

May Snowden, president and CEO of Snowden & Associates, Inc., distills the inclusive approach down to two points. Creating and sustaining a work environment or culture that is diverse and inclusive, she says, will drive an environment that is:

1) Progressive, innovative, and that favors progress and reform; and

2) A place where employees thrive and growth.

She compares the benefits of inclusion to the benefits reaped by regular exercise and healthy eating. Paying attention to the body's health increases cardiovascular and respiratory capacities, muscle strength and flexibility. The secondary benefits, all of which are also critical, include enhanced balance, speed, power, and even mental ability. A well-led inclusive work environment leads to:

1) Open communications that eliminate tunnel vision and chimney structures, just like exercise opens up the cardiovascular system and lungs. The customer-driven innovation and quick decision-making that influences market share and profitability.

2) Employees (the company's muscles) become engaged, and focus on their performance and on building a strong, enduring company. Their efforts benefit them professionally and financially. Cultural fluency and generational savvy are developed.

3) The organization becomes known within its industry for its flexibility and agility (the speed, balance and power gained by exercise). The company leads change, drives technology, and expands margins and profits.

Each of these benefits loop back singly and in tandem to the corporate culture as it recreates itself. Inclusion extends the concept of diversity to every area of the work environment, "including individual attitudes and behaviors," Snowden says. "It leads to a work environment that maximizes the potential of the entire body while acknowledging unique employee contributions and differences." By striving to reflect a truly inclusive workforce, recruitment and retention of the best people naturally follows. The bottom line grows stronger.

Inclusion Expands Market Reach

One of the most important ways companies benefit from inclusion is through an increased reach into various market segments. Individuals who are part of the company's primary demographic provide the innovative thinking and unique perspectives that allow for a deeper penetration of new market segments. Diverse employees connect companies with new customers who otherwise would be overlooked or remain out of reach.

Shari Davis, CDO at CSC, discussed inclusion in the winter 2013 edition of *Diversity Woman* magazine. She said that inclusion doesn't just provide a host of benefits; it's actually critical to a company's health. The continued shift in marketplace demographics requires a workforce that includes people from all backgrounds. Growing a business today means having people on board who understand the needs, desires and goals of these groups. Everyone, from the college pool to the boardroom, has to make inclusion a priority.

By extension, global inclusion provides opportunities in global markets. Francia Baez Guzman, head of global diversity and inclusion at Visa, was interviewed for the winter 2011 edition of *Diversity Woman*. During the interview, she pointed out that different countries have different priorities for inclusion. In Mexico, diversity is about bringing women into the workforce. In Brazil, people of color receive the focus, while Canada and Singapore have turned toward the younger generation. By leveraging internal diversity, companies worldwide attract more diverse markets.

Visa has several programs geared toward maximizing their efforts in this area. They offer web-based training to help managers and employees innovate around inclusionary practices. Their LGBT group created a video that is part of a worldwide It Gets Better movement. The movement is a response to a series of suicides by youths. In Visa's video, twenty employees shared their stories to encourage LGBT youths to persevere in their own lives. By reaching out on a personal level, the company connects more strongly with this market segment.

"Companies that don't focus on inclusion are missing out," Guzman said. "There's a strong link between the diversity of your workforce and your ability to market."

Even when a company values inclusion, it can encounter difficulties with businesses that don't hold the same priorities or that simply don't understand its importance. *Diversity Woman* interviewed Sheila C. Johnson, founder of Black Entertainment Television (BET), about this in Jul/Aug of 2008. When Johnson and her then-husband, Robert, launched the country's first major African American cable television network, they had to work hard to prove that women and ethnic groups were a powerful marketing segment. Their goal was to offer programming that showed African Americans in a more positive light than was done in most other channels' lineups.

Selling advertisers on the concept proved difficult. They just weren't interested if the characters weren't cast in comical, if not downright silly, roles. "It was difficult to convince advertisers that African American viewers were big consumers of their products," Johnson said. "That, to us, was a huge disappointment, and it was also a challenge because we just had to fight for any nickel we could get."

Then BET got a break. The music video market began to soar. MTV's playlist was almost devoid of African American artists, so Johnson sought out videos from Michael Jackson and other African American recording artists. Their ratings climbed so much that MTV started competing directly with them. Meanwhile, BET expanded its programming to include news and public affairs. BET was sold to Viacom in 2000 and continues to be a leader in news and entertainment for African Americans as well as viewers interested in African American culture. Today the network reaches over 91 million homes.

Johnson moved on to a different challenge when she bought WNBA's Washington Mystics basketball team. She had to convince corporate America that women would spend the same amount of sports dollars as men. Her decisive move came in the form of a partnership with Ted Leonsis. He was the majority owner of Lincoln Holdings, LLC, which owned rights in several sports teams. "It was an opportunity for me, as a woman, to get on the inside track with these men," she said, "and own three teams."

Their partnership led to making films, including one about three women who overcame gender barriers to create remarkable changes in their local communities. "Women are the key to development and eradicating poverty," Johnson noted. "Studies show that if you can empower a woman, you can empower a nation. You have to have the confidence within yourself to stand up and just do it."

Chartis, a world-leading property-casualty and general insurance organization serving more than 40 million clients, learned the same lesson firsthand. One of its employees happened to have disabilities. That employee came up with a new product to insure wheelchairs and other mobile devices when clients traveled. The employee had confidence in the need for the product, and Chartis had confidence in their employee. By offering the coverage, they expanded into an area they hadn't even realized existed.

Benefits of inclusion accrue no matter which demographic a company wishes to reach. The advantages of expanding into new markets is so great that Consorte Media does nothing but connect companies with Hispanic consumers and potential employees. Alicia Morga founded the consulting firm when she realized that Hispanics weren't receiving attention online, and discussed her approach with *Diversity Woman* for the Nov/Dec 2009 edition. One of her company's biggest accomplishments has been its work with Best Buy, the world's largest multi-channel consumer electronics retailer.

Consorte showed Best Buy how to reach the Hispanic market online using bilingual employees. The language barrier is big in America, which means a lot of people don't have access to information that's readily available to English speakers. Consorte closed the loop by finding the ultimate combination of traffic sources and creating a landing page that delivered results. The company gained a successful campaign as well as an awareness of their brand in that market. Morga also provided key insights into how to plan and think about this market going forward.

In the course of her work, she defined a key concept: despite the stereotypes of what Hispanics are, they're just as different from one another as individuals from any other group. Members of every demographic have to be viewed as individuals, a dictate I can speak to directly. Back when I was working in corporate America, one of my white male colleagues referred to me as a black woman. I told him I preferred to be called African American. Being the highly educated expert he was, he replied, "According to the U.S. Census Bureau, the correct reference to your race is black."

Frankly I didn't really care which term he chose; both have been used widely and interchangeable for years. What offended me was that he didn't honor my wishes. By refusing to view me as a human being with individual preferences, he categorized me as black. Yes, I am part of that race. I'm also a woman, a business owner, a mother, a neighbor, a friend. I am a leader for women and men from every race, culture and background. I'm a consultant, a coach, a cheerleader. These roles blend and shift daily according to what I'm doing, where I am and what I need to accomplish in the moment. When companies understand that a single demographic designation does not represent the entire person, they truly value inclusion across the human realm.

And because we all deal with human feelings and issues, we can all find ourselves in need of little reminders now and then. My own lesson in the importance of how to address a certain group came when *Diversity Woman* magazine put together a feature called "Size Doesn't Matter" on plus-size employees. Before then, I had assumed the term "fat" was offensive. I was surprised to learn that some of the women we interviewed referred to themselves as fat. Some didn't want to be called plus-size because they thought that phrase was driven by political correctness rather than genuine care. Others questioned why a label had to be hung on them at all. After all, there isn't a special term for skinny women!

These incidents reinforce the need for sensitivity in how we address people. Right or wrong is not the point; I respect people individually. That's the beauty of diversity. We are all different, we are all unique, and we all have the right to expect respect. Get to know people as individuals. You honor a person far more by getting to know them than by knowing what to call them. Identifying with a certain group is "not a marketing niche," Morga notes, "but a preference. If the ad is speaking to some part of you that other ads aren't addressing, then it will be heard above the other noise."

Inclusion Spurs Innovation

Members of specific groups generate new ideas, create new products, and offer new perspectives that enhance corporate operations and bottom-line performance. In a business environment that is constantly shifting and that can be downright volatile, innovation is critical to sustaining growth. Diversity initiatives allow companies to reap the wisdom that comes from a variety of backgrounds and experiences. Issues that present seemingly insurmountable obstacles to one group fall away when an elegant solution is provided by a member of a different group.

Marques Benton of the Federal Reserve Bank of Boston said that inclusion wasn't about counting heads in the winter 2013 edition of *Diversity Woman*. "What motivated us wasn't sort of the Noah's ark—do we have enough African Americans and Asians and women?" he explained. "It was more an issue of looking at diversity and inclusion as a component of innovation, creativity, better ideas, better thinking, and broader perspectives, which would lead to better solutions in business outcomes."

The vast amount of data available to everyone on the Internet has shown time and again that access to a broad range of information drives new ideas and better solutions. After Cisco launched its Executive Action Learning Forum, a program that develops talent while enhancing innovation, the teams generated more than $35 billion with their new ideas. The same dynamic applies when a company taps employees who offer insight into the experiences of a broad number of groups. In the process, of course, companies have to remain open to the dominant groups they traditionally relied on.

"It's important," Benton noted, "to engage in conversation with not only people from diverse backgrounds but also white men. Getting them excited in this enterprise [of inclusion] is critical. We show them that attention to diversity is an important part of being an engaged leader, and that diversity needs to be a part of your DNA if you want to succeed in business."

Generational diversity alone offers unique opportunities for innovation. Today's workforce includes digital-savvy millennials,

Gen Xers with their uniquely entrepreneurial spirit, and boomers who entered the workforce decades before the Internet appeared on the virtual horizon. Generational diversity enriches the workplace through a dynamic mix of thoughts, ideas and operational preferences that is the beating heart of innovation. Samantha Greenfield, an employer engagement specialist at the Sloan Center on Aging and Work, listed the unique values each age group offers in the fall 2012 edition of *Diversity Woman*.

"The older employee," she explained, "might have more loyalty to the company and might be more mature in handling office politics and social situations. The younger employee might bring more [knowledge of] technology to the picture because she grew up with it. So a lot of companies are getting employees [from different generations] to work in groups so they can share those skills."

Of the three generations in the workforce today, each generally holds certain characteristics employers need to keep in mind. Older workers generally are perceived as reliable, skilled, hardworking and networked. Younger workers add confidence, optimism and a global outlook. Many companies are building collaborative relationships across the generations into their workforce. The Hartford in Connecticut, for example, offers a reverse mentoring program in which executives pair up with younger employees so the executives can learn how to use their new smartphones. They pay back the favor by teaching younger employees how to network. The company benefits on a larger scale by building an internal pipeline for leadership as the boomers typically holding executive roles retire.

Gen Xers, meanwhile, have independence on their side. In increasing numbers, they are leaving the corporate world to launch their own small businesses or to work for startups that match their values. At the height of the recession, a full 20% of this generation was actively seeking new jobs. Today there are many opportunities to woo them with flattened hierarchies and a culture of innovation.

No matter which generation or group receives the focus, efforts with every group build a company's talent pool. In *Diversity Woman*'s Nov/Dec 2012 edition, Maria Castanon Moats of PWC pointed out that "Talent is critical in our business. The more diversity we have among our talent, the more diverse ideas we have at the table and the better we can serve our clients. Retaining and advancing people with what I call high-level cultural dexterity is imperative in a global business world."

Market segments and internal promotional pipelines are only two areas where inclusion provides benefits. CDO Claudia Munoz-Najar told *Diversity Woman* in fall of 2010 how she proved this when she applied inclusion to United Technologies Corporation's suppliers. She aggressively increased the number of women and minority suppliers as well as the amount the company spends on underrepresented businesses. By 2009, the award-winning programs had paid out nearly a billion dollars to diverse suppliers. The efforts satisfied customers who asked United Technologies to work with more diverse suppliers and opened up new markets.

"I have a very strong business case that I *communicate internally*," she noted with an emphasis on that last part. "Supplier diversity opens up the universe of suppliers to choose from, which encourages competition and innovation, and it brings us a new range of services and products. We attract very good suppliers that add value for our customers...."

I have always believed that supplier diversity should have a place at the core of corporate diversity programs. It offers minority-owned businesses, many of which are small, the opportunity to get into the game. It helps corporations identify and develop strong relationships with minority, women-owned, and LGBT companies, which in turn broadcasts the corporation's commitment to inclusion. It's also critical for our economy. As the consumer base becomes even more diverse, companies must have suppliers who serve various markets.

Inclusion Increases Community and Corporate Goodwill

A diverse workforce reaches consumers and clients in a variety of ways. By utilizing employees and subcontractors from every gender, race, culture and background, a company proves to the market that it truly is committed to inclusion. The goodwill that results is invaluable. The people who come to work every day also have proof that their unique perspectives are valued and honored. Michael Ford, Hilton's diversity and inclusion chief, noted the impact of goodwill for his company in the summer 2013 edition of *Diversity Woman*.

"The overall intent," he said of their programs, "is to ensure that our workforce mirrors the communities in which we live and work. When team members bring their whole selves to work in an environment that allows them to grow and develop, they possess the necessary drive for peak performance."

The concept is so important the hotel threads the same diversity found in the maintenance and front-desk workers all the way up through the executive level. Thousands of online courses in their leadership development programs cover topics ranging from personal development to finance. Participants develop their skills in ways that allow them to compete for new opportunities like openings, job shadowing, and cross training. With a helping hand from the hotel, they lift themselves up to an array of more senior opportunities.

Hilton also strives to provide exceptional hotel and resort experiences for every guest demographic. The LGBT community has become much more of a focus for all hotels, and Ford says this group is critical to Hilton's success. The company launched LGBT and friends resource groups for employees. They also created promotions focused on LGBT travelers called "Stay Hilton. Go Out."

and "Party with Pride" sweepstakes. These efforts have accessed a market segment with a buying power of $743 billion.

Sodexo, the nation's leading food provider and facilities management company, takes things a step further. Specific and measurable benefits are paid out based on inclusion efforts. Rohini Anand, senior vice president and global CDO, explained to *Diversity Woman* in fall of 2011 that 25% of the executive team's bonus is attached to diversity goals. Importantly, the bonuses are paid out even if the economy fares poorly. This emphasizes the company's intense commitment to inclusion. It also allows them to continuously add to the foundation of experience and wisdom that will help them ride out any economic instability.

The results have been dramatic. In the upper ranks, management positions are held in impressive percentages by women (45%) and minorities (25%). Sodexo's efforts have not gone unnoticed outside the company. Its impressive track record and ongoing dedication have won the company awards from the National Restaurant Association and DiversityInc.

Pat Crawford, former senior vice president and head of Enterprise Diversity and Inclusion at Wells Fargo, discussed similar results with her company's inclusion programs with *Diversity Woman* in fall of 2010. Health benefits for same-sex partners have been offered since 1998. More than a quarter of the philanthropic budget benefits multicultural organizations and nonprofits that serve the LGBT and disabled communities. Accolades have poured in from a variety of groups, including a perfect score several years running in the Corporate Equality Index maintained by the Human Rights Campaign Foundation.

"The thing that excites me most about diversity and inclusion," Crawford said, "is the fact that it touches everyone—all generations, all cultures, all races, and all ethnicities. Nothing and no one is left out."

Tracey Gibson, Director of Global Diversity and Inclusion at Cargill, told *Diversity Woman* in winter of 2011 that inclusion was her personal goal. "I want my legacy at Cargill to be about making changes and creating an inclusive environment where people can thrive because they are able to be themselves at work," she said. To this end, the company offers internal programs focused on gender, ethnicity, and sexual orientation. Employees focus on the work environment as well as their response to the environment. As their mindsets change, they are able to accelerate and grow in any environment.

Inclusion broadcasts true respect for people of every gender, race, culture and background. While goodwill is created internally by these efforts, goodwill with customers is equally important. But a business must do more than put a person of color or an individual representing a specific group on its packaging to achieve consumer goodwill. The best practices demonstrate an authentic and meaningful understanding of a particular market alongside sensitivity to that audience. Wilma Salaverria, vice president of multicultural marketing for Aflac, said in *Diversity Woman*'s Nov/Dec 2009 edition that "A customer has to see that you care about the community."

Rebecca Illingworth Radilla of Radilla Advertising was interviewed for that same edition. She agreed that customers want to be reached on a more personalized level. One way to demonstrate that commitment is to focus on community relationships. Sponsor a soccer team or health fair for women, join the local Hispanic Chamber of Commerce, and pursue other grassroots tactics. That kind of PR and philanthropic effort doesn't have to entail a large investment to generate a large impact. "The return on investment," Radilla pointed out, "is greater in the long run because brand loyalty tends to be greater."

White Men and Inclusion

An internal commitment to full inclusion is a must. Goodwill must be generated among individuals who might feel excluded by programs that don't mention or seem to care about their own groups…and so men, and white men in particular, must have a seat at the table. Although *Diversity Woman* magazine has always welcomed their input with features and roundups, I added a column called Men at Work to emphasize this important point. In winter of 2011, we produced our first men's issue.

The decision to focus on men in a women's magazine might be puzzling at first. But it's clear that we all need to share the hard work of supporting women's rise to leadership and executive roles. The corporate world has plenty of smart, savvy men from CEOs and CDOs on down who help their female colleagues shine. I want every woman to find her best mentor or sponsor…and to realize that the role doesn't have to be filled by a woman. When I look back over my twenty-year career in corporate America, I can count only a few female leaders and mentors. While they advised and encouraged me, they were unable to promote me. There just wasn't enough power available to them to have any direct impact. Every promotion and advancement I earned was guided by a man…all white males, by the way. These men were all great leaders who recognized my ability and rewarded me for my performance.

Too often people assume that white men aren't involved in—and perhaps don't even care about—inclusion. Personal experience and an open mind have taught me that nothing is further from the truth. True diversity includes everyone…people of all races, cultures and backgrounds. To assume that someone from a traditionally advantaged group has money, power or privilege is as prejudiced as believing the stereotypes applied to non-dominant groups.

True inclusion wields power. That power comes from the wisdom of inviting everyone into a conversation that impacts everyone's success, happiness and wellbeing. George Halvorson, Chairman and CEO of Kaiser Permanente, talked to *Diversity Woman* for the winter 2011 edition. "Half of our population–and often more than half of our workforce—is [female]," he said. "Of course women should be in leadership roles. Not having women in leadership roles sends a strong and very strange message about the people who do lead an organization."

We all know that there's work yet to be done. Some men still don't understand the rich rewards of diversity and inclusion. Part of my mission is to help them understand the facts that lead to the highest level of success. When the brightest minds, male and female, compete in the marketplace of ideas at the highest levels, it fuels our companies and our economy. Men have to communicate to other men that, while some women have broken through the glass ceiling, others still face plenty of challenges.

Peter Vincent, former vice president and head of human resources at Time, Inc., said in the same feature article that "Male executives should be beholden to the shareholders and do what is best for their organization. That includes getting the very best people into all roles and not shutting off the path for anyone who is qualified."

Women have to do their part. They have to believe in themselves, speak up for themselves, and enrich themselves by learning new things and stepping into new opportunities. Meanwhile, here are nine ways white men can help women of every race, culture and background advance. These tips were provided by Howard J. Ross, founder and chief learning officer for Cook Ross Inc., for the special 2011 men's issue.

1. Recognize that this is not a women's "problem" nor a race "problem." Advancing diverse women in the workplace is a challenge we all need to address, and advancing talented people from any background is the smart thing to do. Any businessperson who doesn't get that is doomed to failure.

2. Understand that we all have conscious and unconscious race and gender expectations. Well-intentioned people have promoted a belief that only bad people are biased or that biases are always bad. The truth is that being bias-free is impossible. The human mind needs to sort out and organize an unpredictable and complex world. The problem arises when we are unaware of our biases or how they impact us and others.

3. You may know women of color and people from different cultures and backgrounds, but that doesn't mean you understand their issues and concerns. Business environments accommodate a culture that is predominately white and male. Engage in dialog and ask questions rather than fall back on assumptions.

4. Promote mentoring and executive sponsorship. These activities impact every beneficiary, but they particularly impact members of nondominant groups. Reaching out also expands your understanding of people from different backgrounds. Mentoring is a mutually beneficial learning process in which everyone wins.

5. Be an active ally even when nobody is looking. The overall wellbeing of our companies depends on the success of every employee. Find active ways to support people from groups other than your own, participate in inclusive activities, and educate yourself about the concerns, values, needs and cultures of other groups.

6. Engage in behavior that demonstrates your concerns. Even small opportunities count. You might, for example, point out that a man's well-received suggestion was made earlier by a woman but received no comment. Not only will you place credit where it belongs, you will also convey that you are aware of and alert to these issues.

7. Ask courageous questions. Don't wait for others to speak when you encounter something disturbing. As members of the predominant cultural group, white men can demonstrate that women and other under-supported groups aren't the only ones troubled by exclusivity.

8. Take a balanced approach to hiring, promotions, job assignments and performance reviews. Individuals outside the white male group are equally as capable as white men. If they are not achieving success at the same levels, it's likely that the obstacle is embedded inside the company rather than inside the person.

9. Leverage some of your career capital to advance others. When everyone is focused on winning, everyone wins. Sharing opportunities builds a lasting competitive advantage. The organization's overall success will ultimately serve your own career more than other steps you might take.

I want to add one final point. Although I've discussed white men specifically in this section, people from every race, culture and background should implement Ross' suggestions. Too often, I've seen women and individuals from different affinity groups judge each other harshly. Recent studies have proven that women are just as likely to be sexist toward other women as are men. Pick a group, any group, and you'll find this kind of infighting. It's divisive, it's destructive, and it advances no one.

If women and individuals from other non-dominant groups continue to judge each other, there will be no change. We all need to focus on the right way to do things. Focus on the positive aspects and abilities of your coworkers, managers and fellow executives. Lead as you want to be led, and you will lead by becoming the greatest example of all.

Inclusion is Greater Than Diversity

Robby Gregg, former vice president of Strategic Partnerships and Alliances at Cook Ross, Inc., talked to *Diversity Woman* in spring of 2011. He said that "Companies need to move beyond diversity—beyond simple representation—to inclusion where diverse employees are optimized and welcomed and allowed to contribute.... Diversity is about counting heads; inclusion is about making heads count."

True inclusion is about honoring each person where they are in life. Inclusion recognizes that a person's race, culture, background and affinity will impact his or her perspective and their values. At the same time, inclusive efforts value and honor the individual person. And because everyone must have a seat at the table, regardless of how many advantages they seem to hold, men and white women must be included in these efforts. When each person brings his or her true identity into the workplace, he or she bring their best performance, the fullness of their passion, and their unique perspective to the table. A true leader recognizes these facts and acts accordingly.

CHAPTER FIVE

Networking From the Startup to the C-Suite

NETWORKING HAS ALWAYS BEEN an important part of my personal and professional lives. From the earliest stages of my career to my time as a midlevel executive and even during my transition to entrepreneurship, I have powered my business with my network. Through it I've built relationships, gained knowledge, and developed professionally.

At its foundation, networking is the process of connecting individuals who share the same goals or ideas about business opportunities. You might network with individuals that you know professionally, or you might find your closest allies during activities with family and friends. It can be much more cost-effective than advertising or other forms of outreach because it can entail as little as a cup of coffee and ten minutes of your time. You can pursue networking formally through your company or groups dedicated to the activity. You can also discover potential associates and clients when you chat with the person in line behind you at the bank.

Nowadays, of course, you can also network virtually. The Internet has penetrated every corner of our globe, so the possibilities allowed by videoconferencing and online professional groups are truly boundless. Whether you network face-to-face one person at a time or connect your company to others through B2B venues, a host of benefits makes networking a must for entrepreneurs, managers and executives.

Networking for Career Advancement

My networking strategy began developing during one of my earliest career roles. At the time, I worked in research and development (R&D) at a manufacturing plant and spent quite a bit of time getting to know other employees there. In addition to coworkers, some of the people I connected with worked in different departments. Over time I learned more about their roles and how their departments fit into the larger business, which exposed me to new perspectives. I discussed my role with them as well as my interest in other areas of the company, which enhanced my opportunities to advance.

Over time, I learned one critical fact. The basic premise of networking is all about developing relationships. As with any other kind of relationship, networking connections are always a two-way street. Show an interest in other people and present yourself so that others become interested in what you're doing. That way every relationship you build ends up being reciprocal.

Early in my tenure at DuPont, I learned that patience is key. While networking is definitely a conduit for information, it can sometimes take time to pay off with more tangible benefits. While working in R&D, I developed a relationship with a supervisor who was also on the manufacturing side of the business. Back then, I worked at a plant located in Kinston, NC, a small city of about 28,000 people. We got to know each other well enough to discuss our career objectives and a little bit about our lives outside of work, so he knew I was unhappy in Kinston. I was single, I missed my family, and I wanted to do something different with my career.

One day, a position in marketing was announced. Since I worked in a plant, I was often out on the factory floor and my access to computers was limited. If he hadn't mentioned my desire to do something different to someone else in my network, I never would have heard about the job opening. He thought I should apply and discussed that with my supervisor, who supported my efforts. I was interested in the job but worried that I didn't have the connections to actually get it. The position was in the corporate division and was based in a small satellite office in Greensboro, an area I would be delighted to move to.

The department mostly supported DuPont's various textile customers in the area. It was staffed by a group of people who'd gotten to know each other by working together in Wilmington, Delaware, at DuPont's headquarters. It would be tough to break in, but I did my part. I was a model employee and got involved in some company initiatives that exposed me to the higher-ups. One of my activities involved the safety initiative, an important effort aimed at actively engaging employees in educating others about safety considerations. We were supposed to come up with a way to teach safety that was creative, educational and fun. For our efforts we would receive a plaque. Needless to say, with a reward like that, most employees weren't interested. They had enough to handle day to day and didn't want to take on more responsibility.

So I volunteered. I created and performed a skit on safety for the team and the plant manager, which was very well received. I also got involved in the company's quality initiatives. That demonstrated my interest in improving the company while providing me with broader exposure. These internal efforts also allowed me to get to know the plant manager. After some time, I discovered that this plant manager knew the division head who oversaw the marketing division of the Greensboro job. They had worked together at DuPont's headquarters.

The job I was interested in was in that department. Because of the connections I'd made at the plant through networking, my application for the marketing job had several layers. I applied for the role using the company's internal system. The plant manager called the hiring division's lead to discuss my application, which resulted in an interview. Then I got the job! If I hadn't developed that strong internal network, I'm convinced I never would have landed that role.

Entrepreneurial Networking

When I decided to start my own company, I needed to expand my network. For one thing, I still only had a basic idea of what I wanted to do, and publishing wasn't an industry where I had any experience. Expanding my network to include publishing professionals would help me avoid mistakes and conquer obstacles. Since I would run this company on my own, I also wanted to connect with other entrepreneurs. No matter what industry they were in, we would share commonalities, and so I would gain more knowledge from them, as well.

I joined a networking group in Greensboro, North Carolina, called Visions. Founded by a group of successful entrepreneurs, Visions was a networking session that met weekly on Thursday mornings. It was open to male and female entrepreneurs, and attendance averaged fifteen to twenty-five business owners and aspiring business owners. Each session was divided into three segments. A media table allowed budding entrepreneurs to provide handouts about the businesses they were starting. One of their rules was that you couldn't advertise for others—you could only promote yourself.

They also scheduled networking time during which anyone could hand out marketing materials and other information. This allowed businesses to connect to each other for services and products. What really helped me was the third portion, the thirty-second commercial. Each week, a few of the business owners would stand in front of the group and present a commercial about their company, one of their products or a service. Because of the time limit, you really have to know your product or service.

Remember when I said I only had a business concept? That didn't matter. Every Thursday I stood up, introduced myself, and gave an elevator speech about my idea. After every session, people referred me to other business owners or shared their contacts. This made it much easier for me to network in the area because I was being referred by someone they knew. People trust personal referrals, so whenever I reached out, the local entrepreneurs were receptive. They were willing to help me just because I knew someone they knew!

Even better, most of the relationships turned out to be mutually beneficial. While many people were able to help me, I returned the favor at some point during my own career. So it ended up being a win-win...and that's the heart of every successful networking connection. The Visions networking sessions had a substantial impact on my journey to success. I developed so many important relationships and made so many significant connections there. The resources they offered were priceless. After a little more than half a year, I had a full-blown product ready to go to market.

Why Bother?

Whether you are a corporate professional, an entrepreneur, or are involved in the nonprofit arena, networking is one of the most important parts of your professional life. A solid network of business professionals offers a host of powerful benefits. It's so important you should really think of it as part of your career development. The primary benefit is that networking can help you to generate business or client referrals. If you bring in clients for your employer or gain partners for your own company, you and your clients win. You generate revenue while they receive the products and services that they need to operate.

And a good business network can do so much more. Knowing the right people can help you spot market opportunities, find great talent, help solve business problems, and prevent you from reinventing the wheel with a product or service idea. For women, networking also boosts trust. Women still confront various forms of discrimination in companies small and large. Being formally endorsed or having influential people in your community speak well of you can open doors or overcome the reticence that might otherwise turn away potential clients.

I am often struck by the great number of female professionals who speak highly of networking. I have yet to meet one who doesn't find it valuable professionally and personally. A solid business network is certainly helpful when seeking new clients or other sources of revenue. Lori Rosen, who owns a well-regarded public relations firm in Manhattan, clearly sees this value. "From a pure news business standpoint," she says, speaking of her own industry, "you never know who you are going to meet who might need PR services. The universe is wide open in that regard."

Sometimes networking can deliver valuable results and connections serendipitously. "I went to a breakfast last month honoring women trailblazers," Rosen says. "There were 800 women in the room and I sat three seats away from a woman who did fundraising. My client was looking for a fundraising consultant and the introduction was made." The connection she made helped her client keep the ball rolling. Rather than expecting networking to function in a linear fashion, Rosen stayed open to the possibility that networking can happen anyplace at any time.

"Networking," Rosen says, "provides different perspectives. You see how others are conducting business, which is always useful."

Sandra Westlund-Deenihan, who owns a manufacturing company, agrees. "There is an undeniable benefit," she says, "in learning how others in the same arena are achieving new levels of success. In short, networking is the key to personal and professional growth...and instrumental to growing your bottom line."

Central to this view is the idea that collaboration with others, whether in groups or as partners, yields greater benefits than working alone. Heidi Lamar says, "We have a sign in our break room that reads, *We may not have it all together but together we have it all.* I think networking is kind of like that. When you get a group of people-who-know-people together the resources are endless. If two heads are better than one, imagine the power of weaving the best minds into a tapestry that is greater than the sum of its parts."

One final benefit is that a solid business network can expand your business operations or support you during an economic downturn. When the dollar declined against foreign currencies, Westlund-Deenihan saw an opportunity to increase her company's share of the international market. "We leaned on the relationships we built over the years and followed them to new business leads across the ocean," she says. "International sales skyrocketed from 3% in 2003 to 20% in 2008 with overall sales increasing 105% in the last few years. This international growth would never have been possible without aggressive networking."

While actively networking can be beneficial, avoiding any efforts at networking can negatively impact your professional and personal opportunities. If you decide not to cultivate relationships with likeminded business professionals, you'll be at a distinct disadvantage compared to your peers. Personal experience taught me that not having a network can result in overspending for products and services, wasted hours of effort, and poor business deals. People in the know can help you avoid all sorts of difficulties. You're also likely to miss out on potential opportunities. In the end, you might find yourself wondering why you're consistently overlooked.

The reality is that people hire and do business with people that they know—or people who are in their extended circle of acquaintances—much more than with people they've never met or heard of. That same reason drives corporations to set up social media pages where potential customers can interact on a daily basis with employees and brands. The more people are exposed to you or hear about you from others, the more they'll trust you when it comes time to strike the deal.

Steps to Building Your Network

Of course, developing a professional network that offers value takes time and energy. If you take the process seriously and integrate the different components into your business plan, you'll achieve excellent results. The first step is to prepare for the networking process. Too many people decide to start networking without any kind of plan then wonder why their efforts don't pan out. Before you begin, it's essential to know why you are networking. Is your goal to bring in clients, find new employees, sell your business, or something altogether different?

Whatever you're looking for, it's a good idea to stay open to opportunities besides those you have in mind. Before you attend networking events or events where networking is likely to take place, think about who you'd like to meet. Identify specific people or just the company or industry in which you'd like to make connections. This way you'll approach the event with a purpose and a specific focus. And be flexible. Sometimes the best connections show up unexpectedly!

Once you have a sense of the types of connections you'd like to create, make practical preparations. Have a brief (the emphasis is on brief!) introduction ready. Include your name, your company's name, and some information about what you do for a living. Also include a quirky (but not too quirky) fact about yourself to make things fun and memorable. You'll need a good supply of business cards inside a professional case. Presentation matters, and tugging business cards from the jaws of a binder clip doesn't display executive presence.

Next, refresh your social skills. Remember that networking events aren't the same as your workplace. The people you're meeting are attending the event voluntarily, as are you. It's up to you to present a persona that is interesting and engaging. If you're used to functioning in environments where people already know you, chances are you'll need to make some adjustments. A relaxed demeanor and a friendly smile go a long way! Finally, pay attention to grooming and hygiene. If you're going to be in close proximity to people, don't eat those raw onions at lunch.

Once you're at the event, be ready for action and avoid distractions. Eat a light meal before the event. The food served there might not be to your liking, in which case you'll focus on how hungry you are or how terrible the food is. If the food is fantastic, you might spend so much time chasing hors d'oeuvres that networking becomes an interruption instead of a focal point. Have your business card case in a jacket pocket so you don't have to dig through your briefcase every few minutes. Wear clothes that are comfortable and appropriate for the setting so you aren't distracted by being too hot or too cold.

One final tip, and this is important. If you attend with friends or colleagues, don't allow them to dictate the flow of people you meet or insist that you only spend time with them. Be clear from the outset that you plan to network and that they need to look out for themselves. It's difficult to babysit friends or a significant other while making strategic connections.

As you mingle, be sensitive to social cues. Look for groups of people who aren't involved in a serious conversation and slide into that circle. If you see two people exchanging intensely emotional expressions, keep moving and make your connections elsewhere. If the group you're in isn't panning out, simply excuse yourself and look for another group that is chatting comfortably. Approach them and, when there's a break in the conversation, introduce yourself. Treat the conversation the same as you would any other interaction. Be polite, ask questions, and actually listen to the responses.

Irina Lunina, a financial services entrepreneur, takes a very personal and intimate approach to networking. "I always think of networking as developing friendships with people you can relate to," she says. "Once I go to the event I don't like just giving my cards to everybody I see, as I think it's almost worthless since you did not do anything to stand out. I like to develop a conversation with people and try to relate to them in some way."

If you adopt a conversational networking style, it's probably best to observe some ground rules. Don't take up too much airtime. Listen twice as much as you speak. Avoid controversial topics like religion or politics because you never know where others stand or what in their lives might impact their perspectives. And definitely skip the too-much-information approach where you talk about your personal problems, a recent breakup, and other far too personal details.

Know when to end the conversation. If there is a lull or if it's obvious that there isn't much more to discuss, politely excuse yourself and move to another group. It's extremely important to exit a conversation gracefully. When I've been at events, sometimes the person I was talking to looked over my shoulder or at their watch as a prelude to ending the discussion. Treating people as if they are insignificant or not as important as other people is a surefire way to leave a lasting negative impression. Simply say, "I've really enjoyed talking with you but have a few other people I need to see before I leave. Do you have a business card so we can stay in touch?"

Virtual Networking

Social media is a powerful tool you can use to build your network. Many professionals have Facebook, LinkedIn or Twitter accounts they use to establish closer ties with current clients or to meet new ones. Using these accounts is a great way to keep up with client happenings, industry information, and your competitor's activities. Social media also allows you to engage your customers and clients where they are, to overhear what's being said about your brand, and respond to concerns or inquiries.

If you're new to social media, plenty of free resources can help you get acquainted with the various technologies. The help sections of each social network site are a good place to start. Online guides are available from popular social media blogs like Mashable and ReadWriteWeb. For a small fee, a number of local organizations like the Social Media Club, Social Media Breakfast, and others offer sessions to acquaint you with different websites and applications.

One of the challenges is that social media can blur the line between your professional and personal identities. Do you really want a client to see the photos of you and your friends during girls' night out? Do they need to read your status update on that new diet you're trying? Instead, parse the various types of social networks by the types of relationship they serve best. Use LinkedIn for clients and business contacts, and Facebook for friends and family members. If you want to use Twitter for personal purposes, you might want to hide your updates from the public. Or set up multiple Twitter accounts—one for your personal life and one to engage clients and customers.

If clients or potential business partners try to contact you on Facebook, you might politely explain that your page is for friends and family only. You really do want to limit the amount of personal information your colleagues can access because too much information could hinder important relationships. Instead, invite them to connect with you or your company on LinkedIn. You want to be accessible to clients, customers and business partners through social media, and you want to leverage these outlets in ways that monitor your brand.

At the end of the day, social media is an excellent online tool to solidify or begin developing relationships. It's only part of the process, though. It's up to you to continue building relationships offline.

The Diversity Woman Philosophy

Over the years I have developed my own networking philosophy:

- Connect with people across levels.
- Remember that all connections are reciprocal.
- Every connection is made with a person rather than a company or organization.

Connect Across Levels. Some people limit their networking efforts to people who are in a position to help them. They might only spend time talking to business owners or senior leaders at different companies. That's a mistake. People at every level have something to offer.

Everyone you meet is part of your personal and professional journey. You don't necessarily have to build deep relationships with everyone, but opportunity can arise when you cross paths or make professional acquaintances. Most individuals at the service and administrative levels, such as administrative assistants and security guards, have more knowledge of corporate happenings than upper management! Midlevel managers, even if they aren't decision-makers, often have considerable influence on the people who do make the decisions, so don't discount their influence or input.

To network effectively, build solid relationships with people at every level. Doing so provides you with several vantage points from which to assess how you might present your services. People from different departments might come across opportunities you might otherwise never hear about. Connecting with a broad range of people also provides you with access to the networks they've cultivated inside and outside their companies. Finally, when you know enough people at a single organization, you can become so well-known you seem like an insider. Employees will automatically remember you when discussing topics related to your expertise.

Treat all your contacts—no matter what their level—with the same courtesy and respect. Few things can torpedo your reputation faster than being nice to senior level executives and unkind to those at lower levels. People talk, so that kind of mismatched behavior won't go unnoticed for long. Being genuine and courteous to everyone says something about your personal leadership style. It also pays off in the long run.

Reciprocate Connections. Nothing (well, almost nothing) is worse than a person who benefits from your information, resources and connections then fails to reciprocate when you are in need. If you're going to network, be prepared to offer information and assistance with as much goodwill and energy as you received from them.

You might even reverse the typical pattern by offering to help others first. That's what Irina Lunina does. "Networking is about giving something back," she says. "Now, all of us have different needs: some need a career promotion, some need to get noticed among peers...[but] most people we consider heavyweights and the ones we want to get close to already have everything in their career. That is why you need to ask what you can help with in order to expect a favor in return."

Shortly after starting her company, Lunina knew a highly-respected professional who could help her generate clients. Instead of asking him for business, she took a different approach. "I knew a very respected Wall Street executive," she notes. "We shared a lot of things in common and became good friends very soon. I had just started my company and knew that some of his connections might really help me with new business. However, I did not ask for anything. First, I decided I would do him a favor if he would ask me."

She decided to meet him for a drink and see if there was some way she could help him before trying to generate leads for her business. She found an unusual opportunity. "We met once for a drink," she says, "and he said that he'd just broken up a while ago with his fiancée and now was really looking for somebody to start over with. I knew a very nice woman who I thought would be perfect for him and made the introduction. Everything went great with them and I was very happy."

Her intensely caring approach paid off when he returned the favor. "At the same time," she says, "I was involved with a sale of some Brazilian assets and he introduced me to a few potential buyers." Since then, the two have continued to strengthen both their friendship and their professional relationship.

Connect with People. So much business revolves around brands these days it can be easy to forget your networking connections are with people, not just companies. Never forget how things happen or get done in an organization. You don't just get a job—someone hires you. You don't get a promotion—a person promotes you. You don't land a client—someone in an organization decides to purchase your company's services. Your relationships with people will determine your rise or fall, and the specifics of your business with an organization.

One easy way to interact with people is to connect with items of interest to anyone. We all have bad days, laugh at jokes, and get frustrated by heavy traffic. Sharing daily events from your life can connect you with others. Don't share anything too personal or controversial, and avoid stories that don't show you in a positive light. Telling people you were annoyed by a parking ticket you got when you didn't read the signs well at your last convention is fine. Telling them you're annoyed by the fact that your life partner sleeps in the nude is out!

Forge strong connections by showing your appreciation for their efforts. People are quick to complain to a supervisor when something goes wrong, yet they almost never offer praise when someone turns in a fantastic performance. Next time someone has delivered great results for you, go beyond thank you. Send a note to his or her supervisor explaining how helpful the person was. Be sure to copy them. When you return for other business and you happen to need a favor, the person you've publicly praised will be more than happy to help. Take the time to write a thank you letter again.

Once you've established connections, it's important to maintain those relationships. You can use an online service to remind you to reach out to your contacts periodically. You can make a list of significant contacts and write out a schedule to follow. For more personal connections, keep a list of birthdays, anniversaries, or other important dates and send a card or flowers. Whatever methods you use, be organized. It's nearly impossible to manage a wide variety of relationships whenever you happen to remember to connect.

Networking is as much about your journey as it is about your destination. Your ultimate goal is to build your business and expand your client base. Along the way you'll meet interesting people who will enrich your life as you enhance theirs. Developing these relationships is often the most rewarding part of networking.

CHAPTER SIX

Mentoring as the Path to Success

FOR ME, MENTORING STARTED AT HOME. I have two older sisters. Darlene is six years older than me, and Sharon is five years older. Darlene really excels at writing and communication; she has become an experienced corporate professional. Sharon is very cheerful and supportive and often shared her words of wisdom, empowerment and motivation. My sisters helped me confidently pursue my personal and professional goals. When confronted with difficulties at work, I was fortunate to have both of them offering guidance.

My mother was also one of my mentors. We don't generally associate parenting with mentoring, and early in my life it was definitely more about parenting! But as I got older I was fortunate to have a mom who cared about me, and who offered her un-conditional support, good advice and who provided a great ex-ample of how to handle myself in the world. The underlying goals of mentoring and parenting are similar: to listen, provide support, demonstrate care and concern, advise, help strategize, and facilitate growth and development. As children grow into adolescents, parents might find that it's easier to mentor them than to parent them.

Throughout my professional career and now as an entrepreneur, I have benefitted tremendously from the insights and guidance of other professionals—supervisors, peers, colleagues, fellow entrepreneurs, and even people I've mentored. A large part of my life's philosophy has been to help others, and mentoring is one way that I can fulfill my mission. Whether I offer only a brief remark or engage in a sit-down discussion, every effort at mentoring can teach, inspire and encourage others to fulfill their dreams.

Mentors Matter

Some of my mentors were women, while others were men. I never concerned myself with the ethnicity, gender or other characteristics of my mentors. I was interested only in the strength of their character, the depth of their knowledge, and their willingness to support my efforts. Instead of trying to force something to happen, I allowed all of my mentoring relationships to develop naturally.

One of my first mentors was Don Clark. He supervised me when I was a marketing assistant. We developed a rapport through the evaluation process, where he learned I had greater aspirations for my career. He was a great example of active mentoring. Once he found out about my goals, he exposed me to new opportunities. He increased my responsibilities and invited me to attend meetings. He took time to help me understand how the business functioned and encouraged me to learn more. He even helped me expand my comfort zone...I was frequently the only African American person or the only woman (sometimes both!) in the meetings.

At first the marketing team was surprised by my involvement. After I had attended the meetings for a while, they started asking for my opinion. It didn't hurt that Don was everyone's boss, which meant that some people were more likely to warm up to me because of him. In addition to his interest in my professional development, he also invested in me on a personal level. He spent a lot of time with me and shared so much with me. At one point, he even arranged for me to enroll in a Toastmasters course. Having him as a mentor really helped build my confidence and take my career to the next level.

Another one of my early mentors was Ria Stern, a brand manager in New York for DuPont. We met at a marketing meeting when she visited the Greensboro office to give a presentation. I recall being very impressed with her knowledge and capabilities. I didn't try to develop a relationship with her right away, though. I pursued my own goals and eventually advanced to a role that placed us together in team meetings. There I had the opportunity to interact with her more regularly.

Because we had already made a prior connection, I was able to develop a rapport. I started out by running projects and ideas by her and asking for her opinion. This single step served several functions. It allowed me to learn more about marketing, to receive good advice, and to gauge her willingness to share her thoughts with me. I didn't assume that because we'd met and talked a few times that she would be open to mentoring me. I continued to check in with her periodically about work-related things and waited.

As our relationship developed, we conversed more often. She continued to offer her support and counsel. Eventually I asked her to be my mentor. She agreed, and later she became my boss. Because we had already worked together, I was familiar with her perspective on quite a few marketing issues. Our supervisor-employee relationship was therefore quite comfortable. My only regret is that it was short-lived because she was soon promoted into another role. I was happy for her success, though!

After benefitting from such great mentoring relationships at DuPont, I made an effort to mentor others. Around the time my office was to be closed, an executive recruiter contacted me about a marketing position. I was a little overqualified, but it was a good fit for my marketing assistant. I thought he would be perfect for the role. When I told him about the opportunity, he flipped!

Initially, he didn't think he was qualified. So I took a page from my mentors' playbook. I sat down with him in my office and we discussed the responsibilities he held in his current role. I walked him through his qualifications and explained how well-suited he was for the new position. He had some questions but eventually was able to see his work in a new light. And my confidence in him helped him gear up his enthusiasm and his own sense of self-worth. He applied for the job and he got it.

Having a network of support was very important for me in the early stages of my career, and my mentors helped provide it. I learned so much from their examples…how to listen, when to advise, the importance of allowing the mentee to make her own decisions. I gained insight into how to build a mentee's confidence and the importance of not becoming overly invested in a mentee's career. Mentoring has been crucial for my personal and professional development. It also ranks among the most rewarding experiences I've ever had.

Entrepreneurial Mentors

As I moved out of the corporate world and became an entrepreneur, mentoring took on an even bigger role in my life. Mentoring was an important part of the vision for my new venture. When I first came up with the idea of *Diversity Woman* magazine, I envisioned the publication as a mentor of sorts for women leaders. Not necessarily leaders in the sense of CEOs or other executives (although they're certainly part of my demographic) but all women.

I believe that every woman is a leader in some aspect of her life. Whether she's a professional, an entrepreneur, or a stay-at-home mom, every woman has to lead others. She also has to lead herself to her goals and desires. The magazine allows all women to benefit from the kind of mentoring and the counsel I received throughout my career. The interviews, articles and features on topics of interest to women still mentor my readers today.

When I started this initiative, I needed mentors with a different kind of experience. This time I sought out individuals in the publishing industry who might be willing to help. A mutual acquaintance referred me to a one-of-a-kind mentor named Julie Milunic. She's the founder and publisher of *Natural Triad* magazine, a regional publication on natural and healthy living. She was an absolute godsend as I began the process of launching the magazine.

Through her generosity and willingness to share information, Milunic coached and mentored me through all the publishing ins and outs. She was happy to help in any way she could, and even met with me before business hours to discuss my new venture. She shared the nuts and bolts of publishing and structuring a magazine, distribution channels, advertising, printers and circulation. Her advice and support was a big part of why I was able to produce my first issue so quickly.

Her husband was also encouraging. He said, "You are too smart to work for someone else." That was just the kind of support I needed. I view mentoring as an exchange, so I looked for a way to add value to Milunic's business in return. During my time at DuPont, I had developed event planning skills. I was able to share tips and information with her as she prepared for trade shows, exhibits and events. I also volunteered to help with some of their exhibits. Over time they developed an annual event that now has over 5,000 attendees. It felt so good to be able to offer them something as payback for all the assistance they'd provided for my business.

Since the launch of *Diversity Woman*, I have moved the publication into new areas and built the brand into a media company with a variety of products, services and programs. At every step along the way, I've benefitted from additional mentors who helped me launch digital editions, webinars, networking events and conferences. Even the book you're holding owes at least a little of its existence to some of these mentors.

While gaining the benefit of other peoples' experiences, I have shared my expertise in ways that helped other women along their paths to success. When you give as good as you get, you create a win-win situation for everyone. Mentoring can benefit you no matter how much time you've put into your career. Offered to others at the right time, mentoring is always a powerful way to give back.

The Gift of Mentoring

So often we imagine mentoring happening only in the workplace and we consider it only in terms of professional advancement. While it's true that mentoring is mostly about working and less about living, there's a lot more to understand. One way to look at mentoring is that it's a gift to others. While we regard religious giving or charity work as a gift, we don't often see mentoring in the same light. When you decide to mentor another person about work-related elements or life events, you are sharing your time, knowledge, and perspective. Done properly, it's no easy task.

If possible, mentoring should always be a two-way street. Both the mentor and the mentee should benefit from the relationship. But often the mentor has more life experience and a longer professional history than the mentee, so a large part of the process can seem one-sided. Because it starts with self-reflection, mentoring is really a gift you give yourself.

Taking time to understand your own experiences and the role you've played in creating your own life can enhance your passion and motivation. When you synthesize the good and the bad experiences into a series of useful guidelines for your mentee, you gain a deeper knowledge of the events and expand your wisdom. You benefit because you have processed, learned from, and moved past previous experiences. You're able to offer that wisdom to yourself, the mentee in front of you, and others down the road.

Page Ohliger, owner of Time for Dinner, relied on mentoring when she started her business. Part of her outreach included the Service Corps of Retired Executives (SCORE). The program allows people to connect with retired executives from a variety of industries. They draw from their experiences to help entrepreneurs launch and sustain successful businesses. The program functions as a true gift to entrepreneurs. "I have had some wonderful experiences with being mentored," Ohliger says. "As a start-up company, we approached SCORE and various friends and business owners for advice."

Ohliger and her new company benefitted from all her different mentors. "These mentors had great real-life experiences to relay," she says. "Their stories helped us understand real-life situations that can occur and were occurring. They told us how they'd personally felt going through them. These are things that can be hard to get from a book.... They gave us hints and heads-up about things that can occur in business. We have been very fortunate to surround ourselves with people who wanted to see us succeed. No question was too silly."

As Ohliger found, one of the most important gifts you provide during mentoring is your perspective. No matter how smart, savvy and knowledgeable your mentee is, she (or he) lacks your level of experience. When you combine your knowledge of all the situations you've faced with the advice offered to you by your own contemporaries and mentors, you provide a perspective that would take a mentee years, and possibly some unpleasant experiences, to accrue. That's clearly invaluable.

Always remember that your mentee's knowledge can be a gift to you. If you're working with an experienced professional who is changing trajectories, you might find that they can offer you as much business advice as you offer them. When you're working with someone younger or who's just starting out, they might not be able to offer that level of insight. Instead, she might have a better grasp of some new technology or her expertise might lie in an area you're interested in learning.

The payback doesn't stop there. If she works at your company, she might informally act as your eyes and ears. When you mentor people at every level of your corporation, you can stay current on how you are perceived throughout the organization. Any new effort you're implementing or are considering implementing might be adjusted based on this informal feedback channel. So having a mentee provides benefits, as well!

The Cost-Benefit Ratio

You might wonder if the benefits of mentoring for yourself and your potential mentees is really worth the time and effort you'll have to put in. Or maybe you're not sure you can clear your schedule long enough or often enough to perform this task. I truly understand. We're all pressed to the limit implementing our goals and ideas, and making time to help someone else might seem like an unwise use of time. So let's consider the costs of mentoring compared to the benefits involved.

The costs are fairly straightforward. You'll be required to provide time and energy. If you are truly invested in your mentoring relationships, you'll need an idea of how much will be asked of you. You'll need time to prepare for mentoring meetings, time for the meetings themselves, and time to follow up after the meetings to see how your recommendations panned out. Mentoring might be inconvenient, especially if your mentee plunges into a crisis during a period when you're very busy. But as you'll see, the benefits far outweigh the cost.

One of the most important rewards is the exchange of information between mentor and mentee. Being open to learning from others can enhance your career and even your personal life. It also helps you learn to communicate with a wide range of people—something you already need to do at work. Mentoring allows you an opportunity to improve those skills.

Jane Perdue, CEO of The Braithewaite Group, noted that the information exchange is particularly important in a multigenerational workplace. "With three and sometimes four generations working together," she says, "I emphatically believe the primary benefit of mentoring is facilitating a two-way discussion–and exploration–for mutually beneficial sharing and learning. The traditional top-down mentoring model is obsolete."

In an increasingly diverse workforce, mentoring can also build trust across the different perspectives people bring to the workplace. Perdue notes that mentoring "creates trust and builds awareness of the value each generation brings to the organization, and breaks down barriers created by incorrect perceptions." That's why more executives today are requesting "reverse mentoring" from younger employees. They want to learn about their experiences in the workplace and hear their ideas. Executives also want to ensure that young employees feel valued enough to stay.

Additionally, mentoring can function as a form of training. Historically, young apprentices in skilled professions learned their trade from a master craftsman. Mentoring was essential in helping the apprentices become familiar with the requirements of the profession. By working side by side with a more experienced person, the apprentice also acquired judgment in all the various issues they had to face.

Mentoring today allows professionals to share important knowledge with each other. Mentoring, Perdue says, "is an excellent substitute for formal training. Baby boomers can share process and institutional wisdom, while Gen X- and Yers can teach technology and promote [organizational] openness." This doesn't mean the company should skip other types of training, but mentoring provides a less formal way for employees to learn about their responsibilities.

Don't underestimate mentoring's psychological benefits. It feels great to be able to help someone with your professional or personal advice. It's altruistic in the sense that you are giving without an expectation of return, of course. It also allows you to recognize your own progress as you discuss situations that you managed effectively or grew from.

Linda Gasper, senior vice president at Regency Global Transportation Group, Ltd., believes in sharing her experiences with others. "I think that it is very important to use my experience in the industry and in life," she says, "to help teach others. I have been in the transportation industry for twenty-two years, so I have many interesting stories to share with my employees."

In addition to her experiences, Gasper derives personal satisfaction from watching others benefit from her advice. "I enjoy watching those that I mentor grow and change. Hopefully, one day they will be able to apply what they learned through my experiences in their own lives. It would be nice to know that I contributed in some way to the success of those around me."

Part of the joy of mentoring comes from watching those you mentor mature professionally and personally. When they benefit from your experiences, you'll know the struggles you've faced weren't in vain.

Making Mentoring a Conscious Part of Your Life

Times are busy. It can be a challenge to integrate anything extra into your life, let alone set aside time to mentor another. Because mentoring is so essential in building and maintaining relationships, and because you'll benefit from your mentees, make it a priority.

The easiest way to clear time for mentoring is to integrate it into your workday. For many women, scheduling time before or after work simply isn't possible. Your best bet for catching up with mentees will be found during more spontaneous moments—during lunch, by grabbing a cup of coffee midafternoon, or by scheduling short calls and quick meetings—and then sticking to the time limit.

Be prepared for your interactions so you can keep your mentoring engagements on track. Have an initial meeting with your mentee to discuss the expectations you both have for the relationship. Arrange a regular time to meet, and address any other relevant details. Once you begin meeting, ask your mentee to email or call with her questions or thoughts a few days prior to the next meeting. That provides you with time to think through your responses. The meeting will generate a deeper, more useful discussion than if you only hear her questions when you enter the meeting.

In order to give and get the most out of your mentoring relationship, it might be necessary to limit the number of mentees you take on. Although you can always send one mentee out into the world and fill that empty spot with a new one, you'll have to decline some mentoring requests in the meantime. That can be difficult when so many people need advice. But it's better to be fully invested in a few mentoring relationships than to give lesser efforts to more people.

Are You Ready?

When deciding whether you're ready to commit to a mentoring relationship (as a mentor or as a mentee), consider the following points:

- Time constraints. The benefits of mentoring definitely outweigh the cost but one of the most important costs is time. Before you commit to any mentoring program, ask yourself whether you really can be accessible at the level required to act as a mentor or to participate as a mentee. As mentioned earlier, you'll need time to prepare for mentoring meetings, time for the meetings themselves, and time to follow up afterward. This represents a considerable commitment.

If you want to embark on a mentoring relationship but aren't quite at a place where you can commit fully, consider mini-mentoring. Set up a quarterly breakfast or lunch to go over primary elements like how to reach certain goals or how to face common issues. This means you won't be available for more regular interaction, so be sure to clarify that at the outset. You can still invest something in her career in a way that honors your other commitments.

- Comfort with relationships. Next, assess your comfort level with different types of relationships. Are you comfortable communicating with people informally? You might have a mentee who is shy or reserved, or who prefers a very different communication style. Be prepared to interact across whatever differences arise.

  This approach isn't limited only to your communications. Your mentee might belong to a different ethnic group, religion, or some other affinity group than you. Being ready to mentor others effectively means understanding that everyone doesn't necessarily share your views. Their perspectives might align the world quite differently.

  Remember that a mentoring relationship is only as perfect as the people participating in it…and that means *it won't be perfect*. If you're ready to manage both the positive and negative aspects of this type of relationship, you're ready to be a mentor.

- Prepare to think. Mentoring is thought intensive. As a mentor, you'll consider strategies for the situations your mentee encounters. You'll recall your own professional experiences and have to determine which ones to share. You'll then have to convert your knowledge into advice your mentee can easily grasp.

    During each meeting, be selective in how you express your thoughts. Your advice on a particular manager or department, for example, might have to be phrased in a way that doesn't appear critical of the manager or department. When you need to share feedback about your mentee's efforts, you'll need to understand how best to present that information.

    Your mentoring activities will entail much more than simply relaying anecdotes from your past. You'll be required to point out critical elements that an inexperienced person might not see right away. No matter what, you'll need to put considerable thought into your responses. If you're ready to thoughtfully engage with a person you can truly help, take the plunge!

- Feedback is central. Feedback is an important part of mentoring, yet mentors aren't always prepared for this component. Most of us enjoy offering advice and strategizing about professional issues. Sharing feedback, however—especially negative feedback—can be unappealing. It's really impossible to mentor effectively without it, though.

    You might have heard things about your mentee they need to hear. In that case, weave some of those points into your sessions without sharing your source. Other employees might recognize your closer relationship with the mentee and ask you to provide specific feedback to her at your next meeting. You can decline such requests, but you should be prepared to hear from others about your mentee's activities.

You might also receive some feedback about your performance as a mentor. This might crop up during your discussions with the mentee or as part of a mentoring program's evaluation process. Be ready to listen openly. Respond accordingly with actions that prove you value the relationship and the feedback.

Once you've taken these considerations into account, you're ready to be a mentor. If an employee has asked you to mentor them, set up an informal meeting as the first step. If not, find out whether your company has a mentoring program and needs volunteers. If you prefer to mentor students or youths, consider volunteering with a community organization like Boys and Girls Club, Girls Inc., or Girl Scouts. No matter which type of mentoring you choose, be prepared, committed and engaged mentor to truly benefit the lives you'll touch.

CHAPTER SEVEN

Tactics for Businesswomen

WHETHER YOU'RE PART OF A LARGE company or are starting your own businesses, every professional woman will face the same obstacles. In my years inside the corporate world and running Diversity Woman Media, I've probably met any obstacle you might name...and then some! An unflinching determination to meet my goals kept me going. Persistence kept me from giving up on my path or being knocked off it by an unexpected broadside.

Challenges don't always originate in our careers. Personal crises can throw obstacles into our business lives. Lack of capital might leave a woman unable to fully fund a business opportunity at the right time. The need to care for aging parents or an ill relative forces our attentions elsewhere. Some of these factors, whether they spring from the business world or someplace more personal, seem beyond our control. Because of the poor economy, older individuals are having to forgo retirement so they can keep working. The Millennial generation entered the job market during a terrible recession. Even taking on a new career path that will generate enormous benefits can entail risk.

No matter what you're facing, my advice remains the same. Honor yourself and respect your strengths. Know your weaknesses and find ways to overcome them. Reach out to others for assistance, and whenever possible, lend a helping hand.

You are not alone.

All Businesswomen are Entrepreneurs

Ask anyone what an entrepreneur needs to survive and you'll likely hear the words persistence and determination. Ask anyone what a company needs to succeed and you'll hear the same words. Business dealings are never a short-term affair. Every element of what we do in our careers and on our jobs is geared toward long-term benefits. We might garner immediate positive results, but most of what really pays off—profit margins, returns on investment, employee retention and other metrics—arrives over time.

To get there, you need determination and persistence. These are by far the top two elements I've noticed in true leaders. Whether you're stepping into a new position or starting up your own business, determination and persistence are prerequisites. Roshni Phalgoo of Inspired Leaders Inc. points out that any new venture leads us through one obstacle after another. A laser-point focus and unwavering attention will either break down the barriers or lead around them. "Women entrepreneurs must keep their goals in mind," Phalgoo says, "and always work towards them no matter what obstacle gets in the way."

In a way, then, every professional woman is an entrepreneur. Zuleika Cueva of the National Hispanic Corporate Council notes, "At the heart of every entrepreneurial women is the opportunity seeker, the leader, problem solver and motivator; the planner and the creator of vision and mission. We are doers and are by nature very self-driven. We are confronted with obstacles every day and without persistence and determination, we will never fight through to the other side and achieve our goals."

Seeker. Leader. Creative. Inspirational. Visionary. I know these words describe you because you're reading this book. You're investing precious time and effort into expanding your knowledge. You're studying how other women have survived and thrived as a way to enhance your wisdom. As you step into your power in all these various ways, know that the core of our ability to overcome lies in the simple fact of our gender.

"These qualities are innate in us and are a naturally driven force," Cueva notes. "Behind these attributes is something that is the foundation for determination and persistence; it is a power that burns within us and pushes us harder because it's the vision inside that we alone see. It is a driven passion, a belief that we are meant to be where we are."

To build your career with determination and persistence, you must believe in yourself, your skills and abilities, and the vision you hold right from the start. Without it, the student I helped wouldn't have sent the letter that landed her a dream job. Without it, I would have listened to the boss who told me I would never be anything more than a secretary. When we don't believe in ourselves, we sell every bit of our potential short. And once you have that belief, you need to nurture it as much as any other detail of your career.

Cueva agrees. "Your persistence and determination is the measure of the amount of faith you have in yourself. Without a belief and faith in self, *you will not be able to move on and carry on.* Without a belief and faith in self, you will not hear the voice inside of you that tells you to *move on and carry on.* And without a belief and faith in self, you will not come to know a driving force more powerful than yourself which allows you to *move mountains and carry on.*"

Recognize that you're in this for the long haul. Success doesn't come by repeatedly abandoning all your efforts to date for the next big thing to come along. It can, and does, arrive when you selectively choose to pursue new opportunities that will truly pay off. When you have faith in yourself and persist through many obstacles, you will have developed the knowledge and the wisdom to grab the right opportunity at the right time.

Know, too, that what keeps you going might look different than the goals traditionally thought to be important. Lynn Tilton, a woman who founded a private equity company, says, "Women are more mission oriented than money oriented, and what allows us to continue on a path...since we are all going to face terrible obstacles on our way to the stars...is perseverance and passion. It starts with a dream and a vision of something you believe in and care about so much that it keeps you going."

Even if you work for someone else, an entrepreneurial mindset gives you the best approach. Prepare for success as well as setbacks. Everyone will face minor and major challenges, so being psychologically prepared keeps you from being sidelined or completely thrown off track. Plan your one-, three- and five-year goals, and adjust course as your situation changes. Resolve in advance that you'll continue no matter what happens. The only people who fail are those who quit!

Know Yourself, Know Your Company

Along with the key components of determination and persistence, you have to know yourself. This is different than having faith in your abilities or nurturing your personal power. Knowing yourself means you understand your own motivation. Where does your passion lie? What will make you happy not just in terms of financial success but in your own enrichment and empowerment? By assessing your values and aligning them with your priorities, you'll supercharge every element of your career.

I speak from experience here, too. When I first started *Diversity Woman* magazine, my intent was to reach women of every race, culture and background. As I connected with advertisers, companies that might want to subscribe and people to interview, I discovered something unexpected. Industries across the nation that were actively engaged in inclusion and companies that wanted to become part of the movement assumed the magazine targeted only women of color. Because the primary treatment of diversity in American culture at the time was almost exclusively about race, readers also assumed that the magazine was solely for multicultural readers.

This was very different than my true goal of inclusion. All women, including white women, visibly and invisibly disabled women, women of all sizes and ages, individuals from the LGBT community as well as those who came from racially and culturally diverse backgrounds were my target. I even wanted men to join the conversation because true inclusion offers everyone a seat at the table. I found myself filling a need and a market for diversity right away, but my efforts didn't feel completely whole. The gap between who I served and who I wanted to serve loomed large every time I stepped into my office.

This gap created issues beyond my own fulfillment. Because the magazine was thought to reach only a very specific audience, advertising and distribution suffered. Products that serve all women weren't showing up in the pages. Companies turned down the opportunity to advertise with *Diversity Woman* because they "already had that covered." Distributors with limited openings in their catalogues passed us by. That impacted the bottom line, of course. More importantly, it meant that the message in my heart wasn't being heard.

After years of struggle, I finally realized how to communicate my true goal. *Diversity Woman*'s foundation is inclusion. Women of every race, culture and background have a seat at the table alongside men who understand the value of full inclusion. I implemented adjustments to my platform to better convey this message.

The rebranding of Diversity Woman Media clearly broadcast the core idea that diversity means everyone.

The moment I implemented that change, business exploded. Everyone walking the corporate halls needs to understand how their own unique background, gender and affinity allows them to advance and how to help other women advance. By providing answers, *Diversity Woman* became more than just another magazine. It evolved into an integrated print, event, and online business focused on leadership development, mentoring, skill enhancement and empowerment.

Finally we became known for what we truly always have been: the only magazine geared specifically toward female executives and entrepreneurs of all races and backgrounds. This demographic is sizeable and constantly growing. Inclusion is the reason why my company is successful. Inclusion has always been my goal, and inclusion has always been the foundation of my company. I identified that for myself right from the start. When other people, other companies and other organizations were able to identify that core component, everything changed. I already knew myself and I knew my company; other people had to know it the same way.

Until you know who you are, you can't move forward. Any effort you'll make might get you somewhere...but that place might not be anywhere near your goal. Know who you are and what you're working toward. Know your values and how your efforts connect with those values. Once your identity has crystalized, you'll be able to select the path that's right for you. And since you'll know your own identity, you'll be able to clarify your values and those of your company for others. Then you'll also take off!

Adjust Your Identity

Ashley Deadwyler-Jones faced challenges related to identity and values at State Farm. There came a time when she transitioned from a marketing role to that of an insurance agent/owner. Her biggest challenge initially was, as she puts it, being "a boss" or a leader. She'd never held a management position before and afforded her team a great deal of autonomy. That approach soon ran aground. "I wanted my office to feel like this wonderful utopia," she says. "I thought I could simply set goals and lead by example. Boy, was I wrong!"

Although empowering others is always a good tactic, she was inexperienced in exactly how much control to allow individuals as they took on the tasks she assigned. She admits that she assumed too much in terms of her team's identity. "I saw my team as a reflection of myself instead of seeing them for who they were individually and coaching them accordingly," she notes. She had to reassess her approach and establish her identity as a powerful leader. "When establishing a team, leading and leading with authority is essential," she concludes.

But it wasn't as simple as redefining her approach with herself and her team. Once Deadwyler-Jones had established her new identity, she found it difficult to settle into the new role. "It was very uncomfortable for me to own the fact that I was in charge," she says. "I was stuck on the idea that I had established this wonderful team and we were in this together."

Eventually she embraced who she had become. She was in charge, "the big boss," as she calls it. She had all the responsibility; even when she delegated, she was still the one who had to make sure the job had been done well, on time and within budget. "I quickly learned as a leader and business owner you are really in it alone," she notes. "No one will care for and love your business the way you do." That meant taking up the flag of her own power. When she did, she discovered that she'd learned some important lessons along the way.

"If a woman is transitioning into a leadership role," she counsels, "I would tell her not to fall into the trap of trying to create a warm and fuzzy work environment where everyone ends up happy while she's miserable. Be a boss! Set expectations and consistently hold your team to those expectations. As a leader, don't worry so much about being liked. It's overrated. Being respected and driving results is what really counts."

At one point during the interview for this book, Deadwyler-Jones commented that her responses might sound jaded. Nothing could be further from the truth. Her effort to encourage collaboration is part of great leadership but can be perceived as a sign of weakness. Creating a safe work environment in which all team members feel comfortable can be abused by employees who aren't willing to give their all. A better balance in her initial monitoring and mentoring of her team would have helped allay these issues.

As for respect versus likeability, she's right there, too. You're not at work to make friends or share your deepest thoughts. Even people involved in therapeutic and charity work whose business it is to listen to a client's darkest secrets don't reveal their own! Instead of enhancing your personal life, your career and your business are vehicles that convey your message, your goals and your passion to the world. You're making all this effort for a reason.

People can like or even love you. As the well-worn phrase so ironically claims, they can even love you to death. That doesn't mean they respect you. Without respect, a leader can't lead. Without respect, projects aren't completed on time and team members turn in lackluster performances. With respect, your team views you, themselves and each other in a new light. With respect, your ideas and vision can shine the way they deserve. Being respected is what really counts.

Identity and Your Superiors

Whether they're in a leadership role or not, women at all levels need to understand the kind of relationship they have with their boss. They need to know whether the person they report to believes in their abilities, skills and assets enough to trust them with increased responsibility and important tasks. Yet many people don't have a true grasp on how they are viewed. This is another part of identity: the message you send out every day about who you are, what you value, and where you intend to go.

Audra Bohannon of Global Novations, a strategic consulting and enterprise training company, wrote about how an employee's relationship with a manager creates a synergistic work environment. This single element is key to an individual's success and any advancement she hopes to make. A relationship that seems amicable, based as it is in basic politeness, might disguise a manager's true feelings about an employee's competence. Apparently this happens more than most of us realize. In a 2009 survey performed by Bohannon's company, managers rated their direct reports half a stage lower than the reporters rated themselves.

This disconnect can result from unclear expectations and misperceptions on both sides. You might want to be cross-trained in a different department because you see an opportunity to enhance how your project is handled; your boss, meanwhile, might take that to mean you're looking for a transfer. A manager who consistently rates an employee as average but who never recommends ways to improve might be perfectly happy with her performance while the employee worries that eventually she'll be let go. For communication to ring clear, both sides must be invested in the employee's success.

"Maximizing your relationship understanding starts with being direct about what you want," Bohannon said. "If you are interested in advancing, be upfront so you can receive the feedback you need at every step on your journey. Ask for two or three recommendations to help you get there, or for suggestions about issues you need to address that otherwise will stand in your way."

Ask specifically about your performance and listen closely to the comments. Don't respond in a way that will make you appear as if you're responding negatively to the advice. Finally, return the favor by becoming an advocate for your manager. Rather than simply providing updates, make concrete recommendations for how to reach different milestones. "Make a commitment to deliver results beyond your job assignment," Bohannon said, "so that you are seen as a value to the entire team and not just your position."

What if you discover that you don't know yourself or your goals? Worse, what if you find that you're absolutely miserable where you are, but you don't know where to go next, let alone how to get there? Relax. There is a path that leads to your own true self. Dr. Shirley Davis-Sheppard, Global Chief Diversity and Inclusion Officer at the Society for Human Resource Management, offered the tips listed below for the winter 2013 edition of *Diversity Woman* magazine.

- Define (or reassess) your vision and your mission. Too many people are frustrated with their current situations because they have no idea what they want. The vision you build is your promise of what you will someday become. Write down your vision. Identify your key strengths, interests, hobbies, gifts and talents. Your vision is likely tied to things you've been pursuing all your life. This vision and your mission will inform all your decisions from here on out.

- Renew your mind. Negative thinking is a powerful enemy. It hinders your ability to address weaknesses and disappointments. A negative mindset encourages you to make excuses rather than pursue success. Take courses so you can build new skills and strengthen your positive outlook. Use a life coach or mentor who will help you draw on your strengths. Surround yourself with positive, successful people who will inspire and motivate you every day.

- Prioritize (or reprioritize) your goals. The surest way to sabotage your vision and mission is to set unrealistic goals or to become overwhelmed by thinking that a goal is a singular event. Take each of your goals and break them down into manageable steps. These steps are your short-term goals. Track your progress as you knock out each new milestone. And to support your positive attitude, celebrate quarterly, if not more often!

- Evaluate (or reevaluate) your relationships. Most successful individuals are forthright about one key factor: they didn't get where they are all by themselves. Along the way, they built meaningful relationships that yielded mutual benefits. Your network can increase your net worth by opening new doors and providing new opportunities. Because you eliminated the toxic people from your network when you renewed your mind, now you have the time and space to invite positive people who share your values into your network.

- Claim (or reclaim) your success. Define and respect your success. Review your path to date and recognize that every step, whether you sailed through or stumbled, was one segment of your path to your future. Apply those lessons to where you are today and where you want to go.

"No one was born to be a failure," Davis-Sheppard said, "so stop settling for less than your potential and reclaim the success that you were born to achieve."

Authentic Marketing

American finally elected its first African American president. Despite all the talk leading up to that first election, Obama was not voted in by African American citizens. Even if every African

American in the nation had cast a vote for him, the numbers wouldn't have totaled enough to send him to the White House. Support from individuals of every race, culture and background were needed to raise that majority. In fact, for the numbers to tally, even Republicans had to vote for him! That's what inclusion can do.

So why is there such a widespread belief that women are the only ones who need to address inclusion? We need men in this discussion. We also need white women, women who already have an office in the C-suite, women who are independently wealthy, and women who appear to have every benefit America can offer. We need them as much as we need women whose families are disadvantaged by poverty, who speak English as a second language, and whose visible differences force them into lower-paying jobs than their abilities deserve. Women from all races, cultures and backgrounds must have the same opportunities as men.

This simple fact creates a world in which everyone in a leadership position must be globally fluent. That means learning about other cultures as well as the subcultures within our own country. It means understanding the social norms and etiquette of those who live in other regions of the world as well as understanding the unique needs and desires of different groups here in America. Most of all, it means being open-minded about how others conduct business and being willing, even eager, to learn from them.

Inclusion can be applied to our marketing efforts in every industry. In Jul/Aug of 2008, *Diversity Woman* interviewed Deborah Williams about starting her own company. She followed a path that took into account the needs and desires of a specific group of consumers. She'd already founded Behind The Bench, a national support group for wives and family members of NBA members. As she attended games, she discovered that most women's sports clothes made her look like a cheerleader. She'd located a gap in the market for styles that were more mature, a little classier, and comfortable for individuals who might not look like athletes themselves.

She decided to launch a line of sporting goods clothes to fill that gap. The company, called Her Game 2, received an initial boost from her NBA connections. But breaking into the brand-driven clothing retail market was difficult. The industry was staunchly risk-adverse and hardly welcomed newcomers. Her struggles continued until she was asked to produce shows for New York's Harlem Week. Using the models, music and choreography she'd already developed to display her line, she offered programming that was a smash hit. That event led to the creation of HG2 Productions, a company that partners with other organizations to produce event programs.

The exposure that resulted from her willingness to jump into programming has fed her brand. Her typical customers are eighteen to forty-five and predominately Hispanic or African American. Although she doesn't reach out exclusively to those groups, they immediately understand her brand. The clothes are as stylish as those provided by designers known for trendy (but cheerleader-tiny) outfits and offer more hip, thigh and arm room. Since plus-size customers had been underserved for so long, retailers had just begun paying more attention to that demographic. Her Game 2 was right there with the style and fit those customers demanded.

Williams noted that her background in psychology came in handy. "Business is all about relationships, being a good listener, and tuning in to people's emotions," she said. "Listening makes a difference to people and creates loyalty." Because retailers finally began listening to the demands of their plus-size customers, they benefited from carrying Williams' brand. And because Williams knew her personal needs were the same as fellow NBA wives and consumers with no connection to organized sports, she filled a gap in the market. She found success because she persuaded skittish retailers to listen, learn and adapt.

Global Identity

The same approach can transform a company by tapping into global concerns. *Diversity Woman* spoke with Mei Xu of Chesapeake Bay Candle in fall of 2012 about their success with a new product line. Whenever Xu went shopping, she noticed something strange. The same women who wore sleek, elegant clothes to work or during a pleasant night out returned to homes so poorly decorated they slept "in grandma's bedroom." She wanted to offer something other than the usual bland and uninspired accessories so that women could dress their homes with flare.

In 1994, Chesapeake Bay Candle began offering designer home accents to fill that need. The $86 million business now offers a retail site for home furnishings called Blissliving Home. With operational headquarters in Rockville, Maryland and Hangzhou, China, the company has six global locations and employs over 2,000 people. To accomplish all this, Xu had to expand manufacturing operations from the original factory in China to another location inside the United States.

Reshoring generated particular challenges for the company, but Xu was prepared. When she'd been twelve years old, China had been opening up for the first time to capitalist market principles. Her parents saw what was coming and sent her to a full-immersion English language middle school. The experience gave Xu a global perspective that allows her to do business in any country. She feels empowered to make decisions other businesspeople can't because they're too immersed in their own state or nation's perspectives.

Some of the obstacles she faced during reshoring revolved around obtaining all the necessary permits and fulfilling other requirements. Compared to countries that were hungry for new business investments, America presented more challenges. But this nation offered other benefits that were far more important: less bribery in business dealings, more transparency in setting up and operating a company, and strong social compliance for labor protection, fair pay and environmental regulations.

She knew the effort would be worthwhile and pursued her goal with persistence and determination. As she moved forward in the process of opening a manufacturing base in this country, her efforts caught the eye of the White House. She was asked to speak at its forum on reshoring. During her presentation, she noted the enormous overseas market for products made in the U.S. In other parts of the world, a made in America label broadcasts authenticity. "There is something about made in American that is very wholesome," Xu says. "In many emerging countries such as Brazil and India, the U.S. is still about inspiration, hope."

Her efforts showcase inclusion marketing at its best. She took a brand that started out with U.S. customers and found a way to make that brand appealing to consumers in other nations. She expanded the company's manufacturing base into a country that offered tangible and intangible benefits that impacted the bottom line. Her success was built by her ability to understand the global market and how other nations perceive American products.

You don't have to have experienced a life like Xu's to do the same. You just need to be aware of other cultures and peoples, to learn about their values and desires. This kind of understanding can impact your work as much as your brand. In the Nov/Dec edition of *Diversity Woman*, Ria Stern talked about starting working at the Korean fiber company Hyosung in 2005. Although her job was to sell organic cotton and ecofriendly recycled polyesters to apparel makers around the world, she ended up with a crash course in Confucianism.

The belief system heavily influences Korean life and work. Confucianism emphasizes authority because when everyone follows the rules, harmony results. Unfortunately that meant it was considered rude to turn her boss down for a new assignment, no matter how heavy her existing workload was. When issues arose, she cultural sensitivity classes, or serve on a global-oriented task-force.

"Today," she noted, "most individuals need some sort of global experience on their resume to advance." A global leader will demonstrate cross-cultural competence, meaning she will be able to lead, motivate and manage a multicultural team. Collaboration is key along with flexibility, adaptability, and being able to handle ambiguous situations. "These are all skills that are typically associated with women," Anand said. "So this is a great time for women to tap into their natural leadership style and become successful in the global economy."

The opportunities are widespread, especially as American companies are in a catch-up mode. Europeans, she points out, are much more comfortable around the global economy. They are used to vacationing in other counties and speaking different languages. As American dominance is eaten away, global inclusion is required. Even if your company appears to operate only within domestic boundaries, your competition is international. Keep an eye on trends sweeping other countries. Tap into a truly inclusive workforce to get ahead and stay there. Your access is just a computer click away.

Daily Tactics

In this chapter, I've focused on a few of the ways you can lift yourself in your career and take your company to new heights. There are so many more tactics I could offer, enough to fill another book! I don't want to overlook another few key elements, though, so this section briefly considers some of the more important ones. When you implement these steps on a daily basis, you'll super-charge your own growth as well as that of your company.

Teambuilding. When Michele Kang first began her business, she faced the myth that large companies had more resources and therefore could solve problems more efficiently. *Diversity Woman* interviewed her in fall of 2010 to discover how she convinced potential customers a small company could handle complex issues as well as, and even more efficiently than, large competitors. Her solution was teambuilding with vision, a process that continues to generate success.

First, she provides an exciting and clear vision to her team. Using their input, she formulates a strategy that is innovative and futuristic. She then assigns tasks to members who are excited about the vision and who have the skills to execute the strategy. The work environment as a whole offers policies, processes, technology, tools and mentoring that allow her people to thrive. "When a group of highly talented individuals are united by a common purpose and can contribute the best they have to offer," she notes, "success is virtually guaranteed."

Act Now. No matter where you work or what your goals are, you'll face numerous challenges. The answer to them all is to take your destiny into your own hands. "When women know they are ready, they should not delay," recommended Lynn Tilton, founder and CEO of Patriarch Partners. "Men tend to take jobs before they're ready but women wait too long…we all need to find a balance."

Know Your Worth. Research shows that women entering the job market are far more likely to accept the first number offered, while men tend to hold out for higher starting salaries. Women are also less likely than men to negotiate aggressively throughout their careers for raises and promotions. Women Are Getting Even (WAGE), a project that teaches young women how negotiate, recommends not accepting any figure the moment it's offered. And don't name the salary yourself. Instead ask, "What range did you have in mind?" Be sure you've researched pay scales ahead of time so you'll be able to make a credible counteroffer.

Never Give Up on Your Dreams. Prerna Gupta was featured in *Diversity Woman*'s fall 2011 edition as a young entrepreneur. She launched a phone app called LaDiDa that transforms anyone into a recording star. Although she faced the very real possibility of failing, she encouraged other to pursue their dreams. "It's always worth going for it," she said, "even if you 'fail.' The world needs more female entrepreneurs, and the barriers to women [who are] following their dreams are really starting to lift. If you have passion, there's no reason you can't succeed."

Prioritize Daily. Maria Castanon Moats of PWC (formerly PricewaterhouseCoopers) recommended setting expectations for your career and family, then allowing priorities to shift as different needs arise in the Nov/Dec 2012 edition of *Diversity Woman*.

Control Meetings. Studies estimate that American managers could save 80% of the time currently wasted in meetings by running them more efficiently. Peggy Duncan, a productivity expert, knows how to clip and curb meetings. She shared her top tips with *Diversity Woman* magazine for the Nov/Dec 2008 edition. Invite only essential people; others who need to know can read the minutes. If key members can't attend, reschedule to avoid a second meeting that only covers the same territory. Provide a single objective so everyone stays focused. Start on time, and don't rehash everything that has already been covered whenever someone new enters the room.

Be Authentic. Many times women, especially women of color, feel they have to change who they are in order to succeed. You might have to modify your behaviors to meet a company's expectations, but never give up the essence of who you are. Make sure your boss, coworkers and clients experience the authentic you. Authenticity is a key leadership characteristic and will serve you throughout your career.

Deliver on Your Promises. I've always loved magazines. At ten years of age, I traveled regularly with my mother. Every time I boarded the plane, I carried along an armful of magazines. Nowadays, travel allows me to sit back and enjoy the latest issues of my favorite publications.

As the media industry shakes from one earthquake after another, though, it seems that some publishers are sacrificing their integrity and losing readers as quickly as a cheating lover loses his or her mate. I once picked up a beautiful glossy with headlines that promised one thing, only to discover that the content didn't live up to the cover. Promising one thing and delivering another is the surest path to trouble. The disappointment clients, coworkers and bosses feel when a promising interaction sours is almost palpable.

A relationship based on trust is at the heart of any successful endeavor. Failing to be mindful of it means failing to understand the very nature of business interactions. A company must understand not only what a customer wants and needs but what they've come to expect. It's about understanding them the way you understand your closest friend.

In order to deliver on my promises, I allow my love for what I do to shine through. My commitment to providing topnotch information that inspires, enlightens, educates and entertains means I'll never bait readers with false headlines. The relationship I have with each and every woman who turns to Diversity Woman Media is sacred. Trust is earned with every interaction, and every interaction deepens my commitment to always remember what's truly important.

Say No. Many women have difficulty saying no, particularly in the workplace. This seemingly easy task can be especially difficult for Asian women who were raised in a culture that values cooperation and solidarity. Patti Breitman, coauthor of *How to Say No Without Feeling Guilty*, reminded *Diversity Woman* in the Nov/Dec 2009 edition that less is more. When you turn down whatever "opportunity" has come along, resist the impulse to provide excuses or reasons why you can't help. That's no one's business but your own, and providing a reason simply gives others leeway to talk you out of your decision.

Instead, evoke your personal policy by saying, "I never take on other projects when I'm in the midst of a large one." And always check in with your own expectations. Many women take on extra work, overtime, and additional obligations because they're eager to please or are afraid things will fall apart if they don't pitch in.

Play to Win. Jessica Faye Carter, CEO of WomenSuite, also shared her ideas in the Nov/Dec 2009 edition of *Diversity Woman*. Carter is a thought leader and the author of *Double Outsiders: How Women of Color Can Succeed in Corporate America*. She compared the corporate environment to a chess game that requires strategy, patience, knowledge of intricate rules, and multiple players with varying power and mobility. The formal and informal guidelines are based on historic practices, industry norms, and corporate culture.

These rules are rarely discussed openly. Observation and informal communication are the only ways to discover them. Then those rules must be filtered through the lens of race and gender because they are applied differently to women than to men. They are also applied differently to multicultural women than their white female counterparts and their ethnic male counterparts. Sorting out these unwritten rules begins with a well-planned strategy. Understand your company's culture, build relationships with your supervisor and colleagues, and develop a professional, authentic image.

This can happen through acts as simple as grabbing a cup of coffee or eating lunch with coworkers. Discuss books you've read, a sporting event you attended, or other things that aren't too personal. The idea is to share just enough that others feel like they know you. If you can talk about outside activities that have some connection to your workplace, such as volunteer work you're doing for an organization that serves part of your client demographic, that's even better. Place all this atop a foundation of quality performance, and women of all backgrounds can play the game of corporate chess.

Crisis Management. This skill goes beyond normal, everyday difficulties to events that impact the entire company. Shirley Singleton, cofounder and CEO of Edgewater Technology Inc., told *Diversity Woman* in Jul/Aug of 2008 about having to deal with an unthinkable crisis. In late December of 2006, an employee went on a shooting spree and killed seven staff members. When Singleton responded, she arrived at the office ten minutes after the shooter had left.

Her immediate concern was for the grieving families. She gave each one $5,000 to cover travel expenses, then assigned a corporate executive to watch over each family after they'd arrived in Boston. Once the care network had been set up, she realized she was the sole public spokesperson. She was advised to be in complete control of her emotions; otherwise no one would believe she could guide the company past the crisis. "Somehow I managed to keep from crying," she said. "I needed to be strong for everyone else."

Part of her success stemmed from her ability to lean on others. During her first conversation with her board of directors, she asked for a specialist who had managed a plane crash or a similar event where sudden deaths had occurred. Larry Smith, president of the Institute for Crisis Management, answered the call. She listened to his advice with an open mind, asked questions, and then used her own experiences, her knowledge of her staff, and her understanding of the business to make her final decisions.

"You can do so much more than you ever dreamed," she says of women leaders facing major crises. "When it's your responsibility and you step up, you feel this incredible drive to fix things."

Being prepared is key. Jonathan Bernstein, president of Bernstein Crisis Management, was quoted in the same edition of *Diversity Woman*. "We now know that for every $1 you spend to avert a crisis," he said, "you save $7 in losses if that crisis had occurred. You can't predict everything, but you can do a vulnerability audit, create a well-defined system for rapid response, and have personnel trained in the right way."

A company's Internet presence can be an important part of the response. Communicating within twenty-four hours of a crisis event is key. Waiting much longer allows bloggers and online publications to quote from each other so extensively that rumors and misinformation can easily go viral. An expansive social media presence can reach customers long before traditional media can... and can eliminate speculation and misinformation before they gain traction.

Say Yes

Determination and persistence. Authenticity and trust. An entrepreneurial spirit and a strong sense of identity. A self-confidence that demands respect from others. A global perspective and inclusion marketing. These are the elements that have marked my own success. These are the elements that will strengthen your belief in your abilities and the value you bring to your professional world. There can be no greater compliment for me than to hear you say, "Yes." Yes to yourself, yes to your goals. Yes to your true identity and yes to the success you deserve. Stay focused. Stay empowered. Stay who you are!

CHAPTER EIGHT

Attitude

ATTITUDE FOR WOMEN HAS LONG BEEN cast in very simplistic terms, namely how she dresses or how she fixes her hair. It's so much more! Body language, language choices, how you treat others and more are the real keys to a powerful attitude. When you convey an attitude of confidence, power and passion, you inspire trust, faith and loyalty. You command respect, attract business, and encourage innovation. Clients, coworkers and contractors view you as a leader. And since attitude is a self-generating cycle, a powerful and confident attitude makes you more confident and powerful.

We women might wear different outfits and utilize different management styles but we all travel the same path. All women in the workplace establish our own identities, strive toward and succeed at our goals, and make a difference for ourselves and for others. Our paths are as different as we are…and this diversity is a thing of beauty. Embrace your personality and embrace the path it takes you on. Lead in a way that makes you comfortable.

There is no right path to success and happiness. There is no right path to workplace productivity. The only right way is the one that makes you more confident, powerful and professional. The right way for you defines who you are, and who you are maps the path you'll take to success. Embracing your power also means embracing the paths of others. You can grow from and empower one another and build powerful relationships in your office, in your community, even in your family.

In my role as founder of Diversity Woman Media, I've met women from every sector of American business and at every level of success. No matter how large their achievements, some people attempt to tear down their fellow businesswomen. Through it all, I remember this one fact: what someone says or does is a reflection of who they are; what I say and do is a reflection of who I am. Anytime someone criticizes me or judges me harshly, anytime someone does the same to other women, they reveal their own insecurities and doubt.

Professional jealousies are as widespread as personal jealousies. Don't listen to what someone is saying about you. Listen to what they're saying about themselves and act accordingly. I separate myself from individuals who constantly tear others down. By surrounding myself with women and men who build others up, I know I'm in a true group of peers: people who want to empower those around them to be their best at work and at home no matter their background or the obstacles they're facing.

Jackie Glenn, Vice President and Chief Diversity Officer of EMC, shared this with *Diversity Woman* in fall of 2011: "Work hard. Do something you love doing. Don't compromise for money, and don't get too focused on what others are doing. Focus on your own path, and put your nose to the grindstone. It will pay off."

Inner Strength

In previous chapters, we've examined how determination and persistence will take you through the challenges every woman (and man) faces in business today. You've been inspired to step into your power fully and immediately. You've learned how to turn adversity into opportunity, and to bust myths or flip them so they become benefits. All these components spring from your passion. Your belief in what you do and your ability to succeed is driven by your passion. But where does that passion come from, and how can you feed it so that it thrives within you every day?

All these elements can be wrapped into a single component called inner strength. This is about valuing yourself and honoring your goals. You have to know that you're worthy of success and that you deserve to achieve each and every goal. When you command inner strength, your body language changes from the inside out. Everything you tell yourself impacts how others perceive you. When you work with clients who need to trust you and peers who need to rely on you, your inner strength radiates the image and attitude of a woman who owns her power.

Dr. Paula Whetsel-Ribeau, First Lady at Howard University, talked to *Diversity Woman* magazine for the spring 2011 edition. "I believe that women sell themselves short when it comes to their self-esteem," she said. "The idea of feeling good about looking in the mirror and feeling good about who's looking back is so fundamental. It's also about knowing who you are and what gifts and talents you bring to the table."

Inner strength will help you reach for your goals. It will help you define your true self and belief in your abilities and capabilities. Without it, you will sabotage your own efforts. When Howard Ross of Cook Ross Inc. researched unconscious bias in the workplace, he uncovered the level to which women have internalized negative stereotypes. "While men's biases against women are well known," he says, "there is a pernicious impact upon women's performance that comes from their internalized biases towards themselves and other women."

Although people from all races, cultures and backgrounds have to take many steps to ensure their success and the success of their businesses, Ross thinks it's important for women to recognize that many men want women to succeed. It's equally important for women to not only want to succeed but to believe that they can. The fact that they frequently have to work harder and perform at higher levels to receive the same recognition supports the idea that something more than sterling performance is required.

Real change will come from your attitude and the attitude of the women around you. When you present yourself as a capable, qualified person who believes in herself and in the abilities of other women, you create the world anew. JoAnn Black, former senior VP of human resources at Warner Bros. Studios, has an intimate understanding of how attitude works. She has seen many people who were well qualified for a position be passed over because of their attitudes. She has also seen individuals who fell short of the requirements obtain jobs based on the same thing.

"Your attitude is the first thing that people see when they look at you," she notes. "You are always clothed in your attitude. That means your clothes, your hair, your shoes, nothing about you stands out over your attitude." Black was so convinced that she once told an applicant her qualifications made her a great fit for a particular job. The way she was presenting herself, however, was going to kill that opportunity.

"I informed her that her attitude—body language, tone, facial expressions, eyes, etc.—told me she had a chip on her shoulder and was angry at the world," Black says. "I told her to lose it! Regardless of what was troubling her, dealing with it here and now would not help her get the job. I told her to think of good things, think about how good she is at what she does, how knowledgeable, talented, smart she is, and go get the job!"

The applicant thanked her for the feedback. She then revealed that she was frustrated because although she was qualified, she had been out of work for a long time. She was an African American female in a field dominated by white males, and no one was offering her a chance to prove herself. After meeting with Black, the applicant presented herself to the manager of the position for the next step in the interview. She got the job!

Black's advice is based in part on personal experience. When she had been in a new job less than six months, a reliable source informed her that an influential director had publically announced that Black and her department were useless. In addition, the director didn't have much respect for women in management and minorities. "I was angry and hurt," she says, "but that attitude was not going to get me anywhere."

After carefully assessing the situation and her options, she decided that the director wasn't going to move out of her arena soon. Since she wasn't ready to leave the company, she needed to figure out how to get along with him. She decided to meet with him and ask directly about the comment. She wanted to know if he'd made the comment, what had brought him to that conclusion, and what she could do to change his perception.

"I figured the worst that could happen," she notes, "would be for him to confirm that he said it and that he didn't like women and minorities. If that happened, I would at least know what or who I was dealing with. Then I could develop an appropriate and effective way to deal with him in the future." It was also possible that he would tell her why he'd made the comment and what would change his mind. Hoping for a candid response, she scheduled the meeting. Imagine the power and confidence it took even to consider this tactic!

"He was shocked that I approached him about it," Black says. "He as much as said that the fact that I had the nerve to address it caused him to gain respect for me. We were never the best of friends, but we worked together in a relationship of mutual respect and cooperation for almost twenty years until he retired."

Attitude made the difference in this case. Black took a position that was open and direct. She presented herself as willing to make whatever effort was within her ability to change his opinion of her and her department. And if the director hadn't responded well, she would have come away empowered with an understanding of who he was and the prejudices she would have to battle. Either way, Black set herself up to win. Her inner strength clearly conveyed her position of power that day and continued to present her as a powerful, capable woman for decades to come. That is the real difference your inner strength will have.

The Resonance of Attitude

Your attitude is born within you and resonates out into the world in a million different ways. To enhance and support your attitude, consider how you communicate. Every time you send an email, pick up the phone or meet with a peer, you're engaging in a dialog with someone else. Your self-worth, abilities, professionalism and passion can be carried by every word you speak or type. It's important, therefore, to think about how your communication skills impact other people's perceptions of you. Deborah Tannen, Professor of Linguistics at Georgetown University, shared her expertise with *Diversity Woman* for the magazine's summer 2013 edition. She noted that the ways women and men speak affects "who gets heard, who gets credit, who gets ahead, and what gets done in the workplace."

You also should understand the differences between how people from different races, cultures and backgrounds might communicate. The word choice favored by men, for example, is often about control. This is very unlike women's preference for language that denotes inclusion. Understanding the signals you give off in everything from daily pleasantries to communicating with under-performing employees helps you control how your words are received. In a world where phone calls can close a deal without individuals ever meeting in person, this takes top priority.

These days, success also depends on having a global business perspective and a matching communication method. It naturally follows that every leader needs to be globally fluent. That means learning about other cultures. It means understanding the social norms and etiquette of those who live in other regions of the world. Most of all, it means being open-minded about how others conduct business and being willing, even eager, to learn from them.

Judy Ravin, an expert in accent reduction for ESL speakers and people with regional American accents, agrees. She started out teaching English pronunciation to ESL speakers at Eastern Michigan University. When she suddenly became a single mom, she needed a more flexible schedule. Using the methodology she'd developed as a professor, she created a curriculum for business professionals, designed a unique technology tool, and started her own company.

"This generated a lot of press," she notes. "Eventually NPR, CBS National Radio, *The New York Times* and even NBC Nightly News with Brian Williams reported on my work and my business." The success was hard won. Everyone except her older sister and her mother had advised her not to start a business. They claimed she wouldn't make it in an unknown field and wouldn't be able to take care of her children.

"After ten years," she says, "I've not only created a success-ful company, we're now national with clients that include many Fortune 100 companies, NATO, and top U.S. business schools. We have a global reach with multinational companies in Europe, the Near East, the Asian Pacific Rim, Latin America, and the sub-Indian continent. ARI Inc. is now the go-to company for helping organizations eliminate language barriers while maintaining each person's unique cultural identity."

What started out as a way to help non-English speakers communicate effectively turned into a global business. Ravin's experiences with students from many nations gave her the insight she needed to help people eliminate their accents while honoring and respecting the cultural differences that made them unique and uniquely qualified. Her work helping others communicate looped back to feed her business and reach new markets.

Communication affects not only our everyday efforts but our long-term goals, aspirations and success. Ravin says that a primary obstacle for women stems from the differences in how women and men speak and listen when strategizing. Women don't always realize that the way they negotiate and lead can be misinterpreted by men. To ensure success, Ravin recommends building a strong network of women and men one to three positions above your own. You can't count on talent alone to propel you forward, so "women need to get other people talking about them. They need to create ambassadors who will tell their story and talk about their accomplishments."

By reaching out to senior colleagues, women from all races, cultures and backgrounds can enhance their chances for success. Specifically, Ravin recommends following contacts on Twitter and other social media. Study their initiatives at work and provide feedback. Whenever possible, show them how what you're doing supports what they're doing. If you run across an interesting article related to their efforts, forward a copy to them. These simple yet effective communication methods, Ravin says, "let other people know you're in the game!"

The potential obstacles presented by the gender communication divide must be addressed with knowledge and wisdom. The differences between how men and women think, act and speak sends messages to clients and coworkers that can be received very differently depending on the recipient's gender. Kimberly Adams, vice president of Diversity, Inclusion, and Equal Opportunity Programs at Lockheed Martin, told *Diversity Woman* in winter of 2013 about the time a manager took credit for her work in front of board members. Rather than addressing it with him or his supervisor, she allowed the event to pass unremarked.

This turned out to be one of the biggest regrets of her career. Her decision, based in a natural desire not to make waves, was a form of communication...to herself, the manager, and even the board. It communicated to the manager that he could bulldoze her whenever he pleased. It communicated to the board that she was as generic an employee as any other team member eclipsed by the manager's ego. It conveyed to Adams that she wasn't worth the trouble involved in confronting the issue head on. She did learn one thing, though. "It taught me the importance of clear, candid, two-way communication," she said.

Authenticity Bridges the Divide

Deborah Tannen is also the author of *Talking from 9 to 5: Women and Men at Work,* and provides valuable input on the communication divide. "There is a general feeling by many women that you should not put yourself forward," she says. But differences in communication style impact everything from pay raises to C-suite movements for women and men. "To ask for a raise by saying how good, how important you are can seem to many women like boasting. There is a feeling among women that you shouldn't have to do that—good work will be rewarded." As the persistent wage gap demonstrates, nothing could be farther from the truth.

In more intimate situations, communication differences continue to pile up. Men ask questions to gather information. Women ask questions—even if they know the answer, Tannen notes—to build relationships by showing interest in the other person. This can make them come across as an individual who lacks the skills or knowledge to perform well. Women also use indirect language to ask people to do something, which might be interpreted as a lack of confidence. "Once branded weak or vulnerable," Tannen says, "no matter how well a woman performs at her role, she has to fight for respect, promotions and pay."

For individuals from different subcultures, the challenges can be more extreme. African American women, for example, are taught to speak up but doing so at work can rub people the wrong way. Asian women accustomed to being rewarded for staying quiet and having a soft approach find workplace expectations to be very different. It is possible to keep those feminine skills of caring, nurturing and giving. When something detrimental affects your work flow or your own needs, simply set clear boundaries and say no. Cultural divides require the same type of self-awareness and self-management.

Most of all, Tannen notes, "Stay authentic. Adapting doesn't mean burying who you are beneath someone else's idea of what's right. Instead, add to your repertoire with new behaviors that allow you to be more effective. Stepping up and asserting yourself can mean stepping outside of your comfort zone. Have courage and know that you're doing the right thing. Any awkwardness you feel will go away once you learn through success that you're on the right path."

In addition to large elements like cultural norms, things as seemingly inconsequential as your word choices and the type of information you include matter. Let your own style shine through. Offer information about yourself and your approach, your ideas and your solutions. Take a moment to personalize an introductory email by mentioning something specific about the company's recent innovations or programs. When tackling a problem at your job, always provide recommendations or pose thoughtful questions that can lead to solutions. Be proactive and personal in your written communications to set a powerful and positive tone for the one-on-one interactions that will follow.

If any of your efforts result in failure, offer yourself and the mistake plenty of compassion. Then go out and try again! Over the years, I've learned how to be humble enough to know when I'm wrong. People will respect you if you're able to say, "You know, I've just made a mistake. Let's go back to square one." Your peers and employees will trust you much more afterward because they know you're being authentic. Even people who've never met you will trust you when you are willing to publically turn the adversity caused by your mistake into an opportunity to go back and do things the right way. Authenticity is key.

Powerful Nuances

Communication isn't just about words, accents and public presentations. It also includes verbal and nonverbal cues. Cheryl Pearson-McNeil, senior vice president of communications and community affairs at the Nielsen Company, shared her decades of experience in the PR field with *Diversity Woman* for the Nov/Dec 2009 edition. She draws on this as well as her experiences as an African American businesswoman when it comes to communicating effectively. When necessary, she adjusts her voice to make sure her words come across in the right way.

"It's important to speak up and make sure you're being understood," she said during the interview. "If you're a woman of color— or a woman period—you might need to soften your voice and tone. Try to keep the emotion out of it. Deliver the message firmly but softly. You don't want the message to get misconstrued or create any perception that you're an angry black woman."

These kinds of subtle nuances can impact negotiations. In the business world, people at every level enter into negotiations every day. Many of these encounters occur on a level that is far less obvious than the official performance review. We negotiate for more time or a larger budget for our projects. We negotiate with clients for what we'll deliver and the kind of support they'll receive at a certain price. Even when we engage our peers, we negotiate for their time and attention. Your communication skills will impact how successful you are, of course. Beyond that, we need to be aware of how gender differences can impact the process.

M.J. Tocci, director and founder of the Heinz College Negotiation Academy for Women at Carnegie Mellon University, notes that gender stereotypes permeate our lives. "We are told men should be strong, resilient, and aggressive, while women need to be nurturing, sensitive and collaborative." Don't shortchange yourself by giving in to these preconceived notions, especially when you negotiate.

Utilize your strengths as a woman. Enter the negotiation process with the attitude that this is a creative problem-solving endeavor, something women do well. View almost any element of the task as negotiable. If you can't get your first choice, suggest tradeoffs that enhance the value you'll take away from the conversation.

Remember that men value respect above nearly all other things. You should take on that same perspective. "If you have to choose between being liked and being respected," Tocci says, "choose being respected...and the love will follow."

Above all, be authentic: be yourself. By knowing who you are, you'll be able to address any situation by calling on the best of your skills. That's really the highest form of respect you can show yourself. And since you'll project the image of the powerful, capable woman you truly are, you will command respect from others. In negotiation and communication, that single trait will take you far.

It's All About Others

People skills, or how you treat others, is the basis of business etiquette. Whether you're sending a quick email update, inviting someone to business or more personalized events, asking for or making introductions within your network or conducting a meeting, how you handle individuals as well as the group speaks volumes about your professionalism and abilities. And in business, you'll have to deal with individuals whose personalities and attitudes range from delightful to downright mean. Trust me, I've met them all!

One of the biggest issues we face on the job is that one co-worker or boss who always takes the negative perspective. In all the years I've worked in the corporate world and run my own company, I've discovered that the best solution is to create a happy, healthy relationship with those negative people. Never let them see how much you suffer because of their actions or attitude. Always treat them with respect. You'll prove yourself the better person, and you'll stay true to your own values and perspective.

Subha Barry, former senior vice president and CDO at Freddie Mac, addressed this issue in *Diversity Woman*'s fall 2011 edition. "You do not always have to play corporate political games to succeed," she noted, "but don't make adversaries along the way. Try to find the win-wins or simply walk away." Walking away can be difficult when things start to feel personal. Negative people can be toxic, and at times it seems like they live to do whatever they can to tear down others...including you.

I've had run-ins with people like that and know how destabilizing their attacks can feel. No matter what happens, I remember one thing: What others say or do to me is a reflection of who they are. What I say and do to others reflects who I am. Anyone who attacks others is telling you, loudly and clearly, about his or her own doubts and insecurities. Even in the midst of pure viciousness, I keep myself in check. That's when I check in with myself....I understand that I can agree or disagree with people but I can't judge them. We can never know what combination of stress, insecurity and pressure caused someone else to become negative or to tear down his or her peers. I can only say what I would do in that same situation and move on.

Dr. Whetsel-Ribeau advises, "Let the jealousy go. I see this envy thing going on with our [female] undergraduate population, and I get especially concerned because sometimes I have seen the most menial jealousy ruin relationships and leadership opportunities. Women must start being more connected with each other, understanding each other better, and mentoring each other."

Maintaining your balance and checking in with yourself can be helpful in other situations, too. *Diversity Woman* interviewed Keesha Parsons for the Nov/Dec 2012 edition because she'd been passed over for a raise. The moment she heard the news, she got angry. Instead of exploding in front of her manager or walking out the door, she looked into the reasons why she'd been denied a raise. It turned out that her company had a salary cap on her position. She was convinced that the rate wasn't fair compensation for her effort.

She prepared as she would have for any other negotiation. She updated her resume, researched how much others in the same area earned for her job, listed the new clients she had landed, and outlined the additional work she was doing. After noting a suggested pay range for her new salary, she turned the package over to her boss. Rather than dealing only with the person who didn't have the power to make that financial decision, she asked him to pitch the firm's decision-makers on her behalf.

Her thoughtful, balanced approach paid off. She received a raise of $15,000! She did it by focusing on her needs, her goals and her abilities. She also considered the needs of her company, the goals of her peers, and the quality she provided to her clients. Most importantly, she treated her manager and his superiors with respect. She didn't subject them to her ire; she presented her case in a purely professional manner. How she treated others allowed her to succeed.

Set the Bar High

Despite the advances made by individuals with visible and invisible disabilities, their unemployment rate still ranges 50% to 75% higher than in the general population. In Nov/Dec of 2012, *Diversity Woman* interviewed a woman who was partially responsible for changing the way our nation treats disabled individuals. Deborah Dagit has osteogenesis imperfect, also called brittle bone disease, and is shorter than average. Whether a disability is visible or not, she knows firsthand that employers might not be willing to hire someone like her.

Years before diversity and inclusion began being discussed in the corporate world, she'd already become a pioneer. She started Bridge to Jobs, a placement company geared toward people with disabilities. Then she lobbied hard for the Americans with Disabilities Act. Passed in 1990, that single step created sweeping changes visible everywhere today. More cities and towns have curb cuts that allow wheelchairs to easily access sidewalks and cross streets. More public buses and trains have automatic lifts, public buildings offer automatic doors, and deaf children can get interpreters to help them receive a public education.

Considering Dagit's occasional need for a wheelchair and her very visible stature, she might have remained unemployed if not for a forward-thinking corporation. That company was the pharmaceutical giant Merck. They knew her physical challenges would have zero negative effect on her performance. Merck believed her personal experiences as a disabled person would be an asset that could help them address issues of inclusion. Dagit wasted no time introducing global constituency groups focused on women, men, racial groups, differently abled, interfaith, generational, and LGBT members. Each of the groups drew on their unique perspectives to recommend ways to develop talent and change business practices.

Her best advice to others with disabilities—and any woman facing the challenges of today's business world—is don't settle. If a job doesn't offer the developmental opportunities you need to progress, find another way...or find another company that values what you're truly worth. Today Dagit continues her quest with Deb Dagit Diversity. The consulting practice helps individuals who are new to inclusion reach their goals.

Dagit is one woman among many working to incorporate true inclusion in companies nationwide. No matter what your race, culture or background or where you stand in the corporate hierarchy, every person reading this book can make an impact right now. Continue doing what you know is right whenever you're faced with a challenge, an opportunity, or a choice. One day you might look back to discover that because you set the bar high, you reached further than you'd ever dreamed possible!

The Altitude of Attitude

Helen Keller said, "Keep your face to the sunshine and you will not see the shadows." Even when storms threaten my world, I turn into the light of my own power, self-confidence and wisdom. When I encounter negative people, I check in with myself and know that I am unable to judge that person's actions because I haven't lived her life. Every difficulty can be handled more easily when we treat others with the same respect we deserve. Forget about your clothes, your shoes and your briefcase. Your powerful attitude shines through when you know who you truly are, when you trust your abilities and capabilities, when you align your values with your work.

What you say and do reflects who you are. Attitude really is that simple.

A Message From Sheila

Leadership has been defined as different things. To be an effective and efficient leader, women must step into their power. They must display persistence and determination in the face of astonishing odds. then turn adversity into opportunity. While seeking out the people and companies that honor inclusion enough to offer them a role, women must ensure that their own practices are inclusive of groups to which they might not belong...including men and white women, able-bodied individuals, and those who seem to have every benefit already within reach.

At its core, leadership comes down to two elements: the respect you offer yourself and the respect you offer others. You must respect your abilities and capabilities enough to negotiate for the rewards that reflect your true worth. You must honor your needs, goals and desires enough to chart your course and then step onto that path. The woman who can do this while offering the same respect to her peers, coworkers, mentors and sponsors is a great and powerful leader even if she doesn't hold an official title.

Differentiate yourself by staying positive. Too many negative people, opinions and commentaries are floating around in our professional lives these days. Do be aware of others' mistakes and learn from them, but never criticize others in a public or professional realm. The proper time and place to discuss someone's faltering steps is in a small personal setting. You can learn from another's errors when you discuss the event with girlfriends after dinner over a glass of wine. Whether you're voicing praise or confronting conflict, the key to handling it properly is to exercise dignity and respect. The women around you who have achieved success lead due to the hard work and extra effort they expended to achieve their goals.

Even if someone else seems to have coasted easily along his or her entire career, you have no idea what he or she might be dealing with in his or her personal lives or even what goes on behind corporate doors. Stay focused on your own career, your own life, your own goals. Stay in your own lane! Ask yourself only what you need to do to advance…and then ignore the drama other people are entangled in. Keep your attention and your efforts focused only on your own path, and you'll fly down that road faster than ever before.

When negative events crop up in your arena, deal with the ones that demand attention. If something will adversely affect your career, your company, your professional reputation or your team, approach it with a calm, capable demeanor. Everything else put aside. If you're unsure whether something requires your attention, judge your return on investment. Is it worth the ROI you will achieve to fight this battle? If not, put your time, talent and energy into something that will.

If you are reading this, then chances are I already know a few things about you. I would describe you as a leader. You might come from any race or background but you seek to make a difference in your organization, your community and your world. You are strong, influential, and passionate about success. While seeking resources and tools to achieve your life goals, you're also willing to mentor others so they can reach their goals. You seek a level playing field for yourself and all women.

And you're making a difference. Women represent over 50% of the workforce, and the percentage of women in leadership positions is growing every day. From 2000 to 2010, the number of women who were officers in Fortune 500 companies rose from 11.2% to 15.7 percent. Today's younger women have reversed the education gap by holding degrees at higher rates than their male peers. Globally, women in cultures that are heavily paternalistic are defying tradition and even their country's laws by entering the job market.

Unfortunately, the progress we've made to date has been slow. At the rates we've seen over the previous decades, it will take forty years for the ratio of women in the C-suite to match the number of men. Everything I do is geared toward supercharging the speed of women's advancement. Together we will grow a community of powerful female leaders from every race, culture and background. Together we will help smart, savvy businesswomen achieve their career and business goals. Together we will make an impact. Together, I have no doubt that we can change the world.

Change is already here. Near the end of 2012, Diversity Woman Media sponsored its seventh annual business leadership conference. Safety concerns surrounding Hurricane Sandy forced us to postpone the conference to the week before Christmas. Although rescheduling and having the new date fall so near the holidays might have caused a significant drop in attendance, over 500 women flocked in from across the country! The success of the conference that year reflected the significance of the women's leadership movement in American consciousness and the marketplace. So many women and our male allies said, "Come hell or high water (literally), I wouldn't miss it!"

As the country's leading diversity and leadership experts swirled around me, I realized how important Diversity Woman Media's role is in bringing together these thought and action leaders. I also realized what a responsibility I have. In just nine short years, the conference and the magazine has become one of the hubs of the leadership landscape for women of all races, cultures and backgrounds. As the best ideas bubble to the top and are put into action, it is our responsibility to be the incubator and spread the word.

One of my inspirations for launching the Diversity Woman brand was the lack of leadership development opportunities for women in corporate America. I discovered this disparity after having been displaced from a Fortune 500 company that had supported leadership development for everyone. I quickly learned that their approach was anything but typical. Now companies are taking leadership development for women seriously. I am proud and honored that *Diversity Woman* magazine has been part of that change. Our goal is to promote leadership and executive development for women at our conferences and through our digital properties like the newsletter available at *www.DiversityWoman.com*.

My company arrived at the forefront of the movement to develop more female leaders and executives by maintaining a direct focus on leadership development, ideas, solutions and resources to help you advance in your career. For now, the most important message I want you to take away from this book is:

What you say or do is a reflection of who you are
What someone else says or does is a reflection of who they are

I personally think that we can react or respond to anything with blame. We're all human, and we all deal with a number of stressors, problems and issues every day. When you find yourself under attack or are present when an associate attacks someone else, remember that who they are, is not who you are. Knowing this, we can stand firm without stooping to someone else's level. We are bigger people when we stay true to ourselves. We should not let someone else's action move us away from what's right. We can defend ourselves and respond to any situation in a professional manner. Follow your heart. Do what you know is right!

While reading this book, you've encountered women from a variety of races, cultures and backgrounds. You've heard from men who are actively supporting women in their career goals throughout the corporate world. You've seen young entrepreneurs reach for their dreams and women stride into the C-suite. Now I challenge you to pursue your dreams, the things that at this moment are only visions.

We can find all the excuses in the world why we can't do something. Starting today, let's find all the excuses in the world why we should make those dreams and visions real. When I first had my vision for *Diversity Woman* magazine, I shared my idea with a friend. She thought I should explore that option. But publishing a magazine didn't fit my concept of how I could support myself. Months later, I found myself frustrated and disappointed by a fruitless job search. My friend said that maybe God was trying to give me the opportunity to explore my vision. I told her she was crazy. I didn't have enough money to start a business, let alone invest in a magazine.

She challenged me deeply by saying, "That's what is wrong with women today. We always find a reason we can't explore an idea." When a man has an idea, the last thing he thinks about is where the money is going to come from. Besides, she hadn't said to run right out and do it. She had suggested that I explore the idea to see if it was really the right path for me. It was exactly the message that would challenge me to do just that. Fast-forward to today and just look at where I am!

Take your chances. Know your strengths. Believe in your abilities, and banish forever the myth that women have to be the b-word to make it in business. Great women do not have to lead like men. Be yourself. Be authentic and be a great leader who just happens to be a woman. So step into your power and at all times, lead by example!

About the Author

Sheila Robinson is a visionary leader whose passion lies in supporting the professional development of women of all races, cultures and backgrounds. The magazine she launched in 2004, Diversity Woman, provides the tools women need to excel with their businesses and succeed in their careers. She offers over twenty years of experience in corporate America in roles ranging from project management to global marketing. As an entrepreneur, she offers knowledge and wisdom to small business owners and start-ups to ease their path. Her broad range of experience empowers, educates and enhances every step taken by women as diverse as recent college graduates to C-suite executives. For women who mean business, Sheila leads the charge.

Go to DiversityWoman.com
to Get the Magazine!

CPSIA information can be obtained
at www.ICGtesting.com
Printed in the USA
FFOW05n0921070714